Chaos, Synchronicity, and Capitalism:
The Phases in the Evolution of a Natural System

Chaos, Synchronicity, and Capitalism:

The Phases in the Evolution of a Natural System

ISBN 978-0-6151-5190-8

Arthur Jackson
4708 87th Street S.W.
Mukilteo, WA

PRINTED IN THE UNITED STATES OF AMERICA.

Table of Contents

List of Illustrations and Tables

Preface

This is a work of associated theories which lead to what I believe is a different and more enlightened view of an old system that has existed for thousands of years and continues to work in conjunction with humanity and life in general on this planet.

Introduction

Capitalism has been defined in many ways throughout the ages. These descriptions range from the traditional American model espoused by Adam Smith in his classical work, *The Wealth of Nations*, to the more political model of Ellen Meiksens Wood in her book, *The Origin of Capitalism*. In recent years, we have begun to understand that Capitalism has existed with mankind for a longer period of time than earlier believed, dating back some 1100 years. Its origins are found in natural systems arising out of the beginning of farming rather than manmade economic systems. It is perhaps this more recent understanding of Capitalism that has drawn us closer to its true nature. These facts offer what I believe are novel and unique insights into the true nature of Capitalism. The first concept is the work of Ellen Meiksens Wood which moves Capitalism further back in the time stream with ties to the beginnings of human farming. The second is the thought provoking and ground-breaking work of Richard Dawkins, *The Selfish Gene*, which states that there exists a psychological equivalent of genes which he calls "*memes*." These psychological packets are ways of transmitting ideas and propagating them through human culture. Next are the emerging science of Chaos Theory and the study of complex non-linear systems. The final piece of the puzzle was the development of a new science to study the emergence of spontaneous order occurring in our universe. This study of synchrony is called "Sync."

The first of these developments deals with connecting the origins of Capitalism to the start of human agriculture. By creating this connection between farming and Capitalism, for the first time we can see the conditions for the creation of this natural system tied to surplus. It is in the study of the creation of surplus and how it was handled in these small communities as they struggled to make the change from nomadic existence to stable farming communities that we begin to see the emergence of the natural system: Capitalism. It is the creation of these communities which is important and critical to this viewpoint. Yet, without understanding the mechanisms by which this system has been able to transmit itself, and therefore spread itself to much of human culture, we lose an important context for Capitalism. In real terms, Capitalism is a system, and it has spread throughout human civilization. Richard Dawkins first touched upon the mechanism for this transmission in his discussion of *memes*. The idea that there are psychological packets which can be transmitted in the same fashion as biological genes helps tremendously in the understanding of why Capitalism would spread so ruthlessly when other systems have failed. But, knowing the existence of a thing and how it might have propagated itself is meaningless unless we can understand its essentials nature. This final piece falls into place when we began to look at Capitalism in light of the new science of synchronous behavior discussed by Steven Strogatz in his book *Sync*. Here for the first time, we have all the tools necessary to do an analysis of Capitalism in a manner that ignores the artificial distinction between biological systems, social systems, and physical systems. By using the science of synchronous behavior, we can begin to understand how this system, Capitalism, functions, propagates itself, and has been able to spread and survive without concern for political systems, geographical location, or culture.

This new perspective will help to answer four fundamental questions about capitalism. The first is if Capitalism is a natural system. The second question then immediately follows: how has the system affected human behavior? Capitalism as a system has had a significant impact upon human beings and their culture; defining those impacts and their resultant effects is important. The result of these impacts has been to move humanity to respond in synchronous behavior with the system. Because we as humans have become so synchronized with this system, where the system goes we must follow. This leads to the next question of where is the system taking us. As a system, it evolves and changes over time. If we accept this hypothesis, then we need to consider where the system is leading us. This will of course lead to the last question, as to whether the system controls people or if people control the system. This final question is critical to understanding how we can affect change within this system and ultimately determine where we want the system to go and how it will take us there.

Part I

The Small Ripple Begins

Farming and Surplus: The Start of a Natural System

I started this journey with the opening of a book, *Women in Prehistory* by Margaret Ehrenberg. It was a fascinating look into the early stages of human development. Her focus was on the relationship of women in early human development, but it led me to several questions about human social systems and one system in particular: Capitalism. What was it? Where did it start? These two questions took me on a journey from the end of an ice age to modern theories in today's world. As with all things, we should start at the beginning: the end of the Ice Age.

At the end of the last Ice Age, some 15,000 years ago, humanity was struggling for survival. This tenuous existence consisted of wandering in groups and forging for what ever the land would provide. This was not a noble existence, but it was enough to sustain the species. There was no permanence; there was only the day to day struggle to survive. Such was the existence of humanity.

Sometime between 11,000 and 6,000 thousand years B.C.E., there was a significant change in the human condition. Suddenly, humanity moved from their nomadic existence as a forger and gatherer, to becoming farmers. Recent studies on the origins of farming by Mellaart and Bender support this. It was, however, Margaret Ehrenberg that provided the most comprehensive discussion on the start of farming.

As Ehrenberg points out in her book, *Women in Prehistory*, published by the University of Oklahoma Press in 1989, the transition from foraging to farming marks the change of humanities movement from the Old and Middle Stone Ages to the new Stone Age. There were tremendous strides by archaeologists in discovering when and where agriculture first came about, and some of the stages which occurred in the transition from being a forging society to that of a stable farming society. Radiocarbon dating has established the dates when humanity was fully engaged in agriculture as this time period. It started in the Fertile Crescent, a valley in the Middle East, and moved gradually into Europe and Southwest Asia.

The Fertile Crescent was a place of fertile soil and temperate climate. Here, wild grain could be found in abundance. Groups of humans found this region ideal for foraging for the next several hundred years. They became dependent upon these seasonal crops of grains as they moved from site to site, collecting food. It was these grains (wheat, wild grasses, etc.) which would sustain the human foragers during this time. These groups were not vegetarian; they would have supplemented their diet with game whenever possible. However, the hunting of game was always an uncertain proposition. For every successful hunt, there would be many unsuccessful ones. In fact, the population of large mammals was on the decrease after the last Ice Age. Because of the shortage of meat, these early human's main source of food would be plants and grains. They would locate a desirable patch of grains in one season and would return in the next few to the same location by happenstance. Over many seasons, this pattern would begin to repeat, as the grains would be found in the same areas each season.

Over time, this recurring activity of gathering grains in the same areas for food sources became important. Ehrenberg points out these grains would provide the bulk of the diet for most of the groups of forgers, making them an increasingly important source of food. By studying other groups of nomadic foragers still in existence today in places such as New Guinea and parts of Africa, Ehrenberg was able to conclude that it was possible for these groups of wandering humans to move beyond simple foraging to a rudimentary form of farming horticulture. There would have been recurring activity centered on certain grains, and after many repetitious cycles, humans would have begun to recognize the importance of these grains as a food source. The location where these grains grew became important in locating game animals that would likewise use the grains for food. These two items would eventually lead to groups staying in the general vicinity of these grain sources and eventually working out how to develop and grow the grains on their own.

Conversely, there would have come the next small step: the domestication of animals. Domestication of animals was a key factor in the development of human culture. In the regions of the Fertile Crescent and Asia, domestication began thousands of years before it did in other parts of the world. The dog, sheep, and goat would prove suitable for domestication in this region for many reasons: they were plentiful; they were omnivores, easily adjusting to a variety of feeds; they were amenable to captive breeding and grew relatively quickly; and they had disposition that were easily adoptable to being around humans .These early small mammals would prove very important in the overall development of farming.

Domestic animals were only a minor part of the farming package. Plant cultivation was the essential part; being able to grow certain plants was critical in providing food for humans and their newly-domesticated animals. Again, Ehrenberg saw the same pattern in certain cultures that operate using similar farming horticulture principles today. Years of trial and error would show these primitive humans which grains were most useful to them. They would soon begin the slow process from gathering wild plants to experimenting with cultivating their own. They would start to clear areas of land for the planting of crops. This process would not require the use of anything other than simple hand tools. Over time, the cultivation of plants and small groups of animals in domestication would be the kernel that would lead to successful farming.

Fertile Crescent

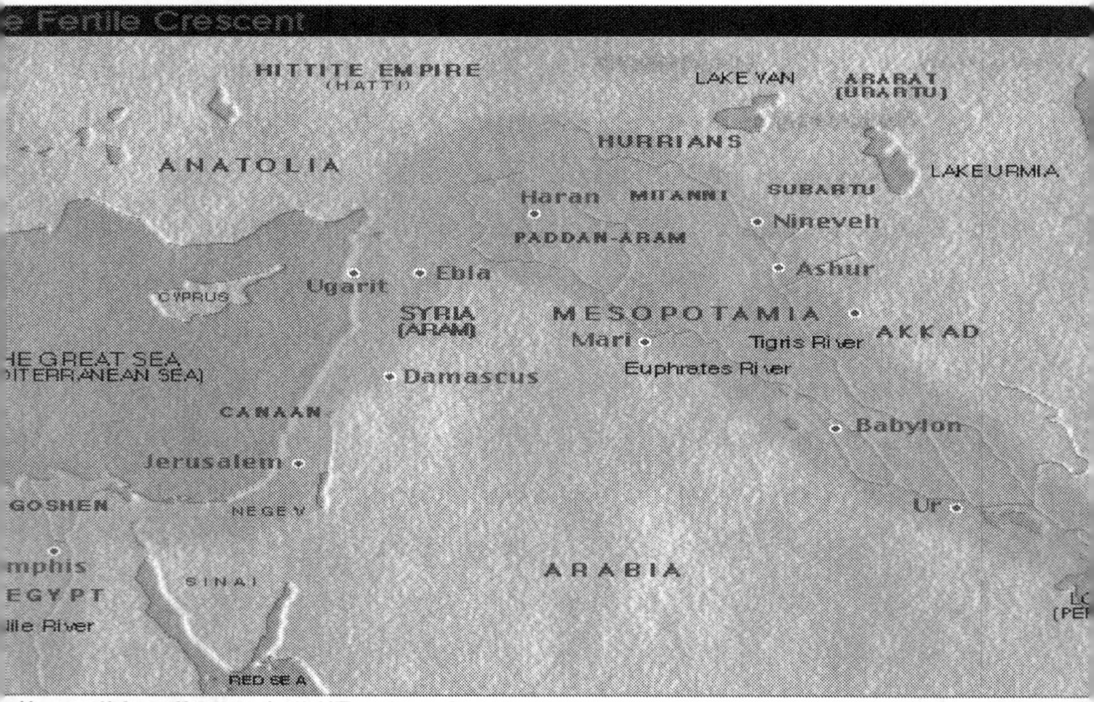

://en.wikipedia.org/wiki/Fertile_Crescent

This is a theme that we will see repeated in much of human evolution: recurring patterns of activity that gradually organize themselves into a system of behavior. It doesn't take much imagination to see the groups of wandering humans gathering on a routine basis around recurring stands of grains. Ehrenberg indicates that after many summers of repeating this activity, they would begin to form a pattern of behavior centered on these plants. This would be the beginnings of cultivation. However, cultivation would mean that they would also have to stay in close proximity to these plants to protect them from animals as well as other groups of humans. Hence, we see the first formative relationships between humans and property beginning to form. By taking care of the plants, there were insuring that their group would have continuous food stores throughout the next year. A stable food source would mean a resulting increase in population. We have a recurring cycle of activity, developing out of a chaotic mix. The results are the modification of human activity. It would effectively move humanity to change the way it obtained food. There would also be other changes. To care for these crops would require a fundamental shift in the structure of the group of humans: there would be a need for shelter near the crops; there would need to be decisions about the distribution of work and the types of work to be preformed; most importantly, there would be the decision about this group's relationship to other groups in the area. One site might see a mixture of hunter-gathers and fledgling farmers as competition not just for food, but for all important water. How would these conflicts be resolved?

Enter Chaos and Sync

While I considered these complex patterns of behavior, my mind wandered back to readings from a book by James Gleick, *Chaos: Making a New Science*, published by Penguin Press, 1989. Chaos theory is the study of complex patterns in non-linear systems, which are abundant in nature. The study of these complex patterns has led to a number of breakthroughs in many different areas of science from mathematics, physics, biology, medicine, and social science. Chaos theory deals with making connections between different kinds of irregularities.

The first formulations of this theory were by Ed Lorenz. Lorenz was involved in the new science of predicting weather, or meteorology. He had constructed a mathematical model to be used on computers to predict patterns of weather development. The model he constructed was limited, as were the computers available for use at that time. In order to better understand the mathematical models he had built and the output of data from the computer, he created a method of graphing the data. These graphs allowed him a visual representation to better understand how the system he was modeling worked. One day in 1961, he was working on an analysis of a particularly long problem and rather than waiting for the entire set of calculations, he decided to create a shortcut. He input data into the model at an intermediate point and set the process in motion. While the computer was working on crunching the numbers, he went down the hallway to get himself a cup of coffee. When he returned, what he saw perplexed him. The output from the machine did not duplicate his earlier rounds of calculations with same data; it was different. He quickly reviewed the steps he had taken while inputting the data. In addition to starting an intermediate point, he had rounded off the numbers to save time. The result was a pattern that showed the mathematical models he was running on the computer were diverging from his previous output. After engaging in some investigation to be sure that there was no malfunction of the model or the computer, he realized that something new was happening. The small round-off errors he had introduced into the system were behaving very much like miniscule inputs did in real nature. Small changes would often create major changes after much iteration in systems. He wrote a paper describing his findings which languished in the vaults of science for many years. The output of this model and the strange image it created became known as the "Lawrence attractor." In decades to follow, as the scientific community began to embrace and understand chaos theory, the study of patterns of behavior in disorder, the image created by Lorenz, which resembled a butterfly's wings, became the symbol for the study of complex nonlinear systems in the real world.

Lorenz Attractor

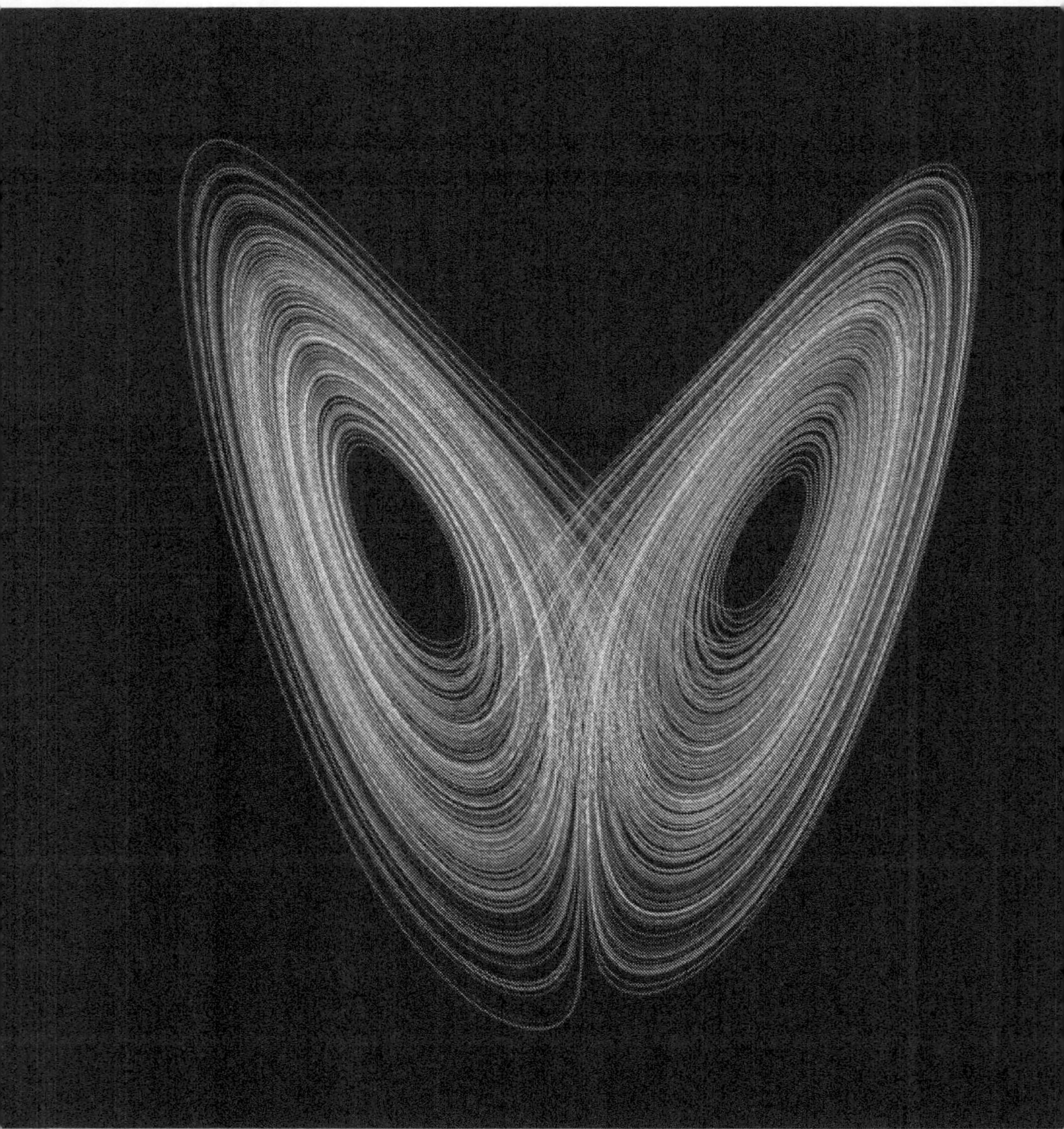

This is a file from the Wikimedia Commons. The description on its description page there is shown below.

An icon of chaos theory - the Lorenz attractor.

Projection of trajectory of Lorenz system in phase space with "canonical" values of parameters r=28, σ = 10, b = 8/3 (or 2.666667) and integration time step 0.001.

Computed in Fractint by Wikimol (25.5.2005)

In the years that would follow, others such as the mathematicians Stephen Smale and James York would discover the work of Lorenz and incorporate the findings into their own work. York, who considered himself a philosopher as well as a mathematician, is sometimes credited with giving Chaos Theory its name. While working for an interdisciplinary department at the University of Maryland called the Institute for Physical Science and Technology, he was given an unusual degree of freedom which allowed him frequent contact with a wide range of disciplines. It was during this time in 1972 when he first read Lorenz's 1963 paper, "Determinist Non Periodic Flow." York realized that physicists had learned not to see chaos but to look instead for order; they were concentrating instead on the solvable systems that could be easily written down and explained. York noticed that the universe is full of disorder and that people need to know about disorder if they are to understand and deal with it. He was beginning to understand the nature of complexity. As a result of his studies, he wrote a paper titled, "Period Three Implies Chaos" which was meritorious in itself, but is also where the name Chaos originated.

It would take an even more unusual viewpoint, as James Gleick points out in his book *Chaos*, to bring the full beauty and understanding of Chaos Theory into mainstream science. Benoit Mandelbrot had that needed viewpoint. Mandelbrot was a jack of all trades in mathematics working for the International Business Machines Corp. He was to eventually create a visual concept that would help the scientific community and the general public understand that in the most disorderly mountains of data dwelt an unexpected kind of order or pattern. This began as the study of a real problem while working at IBM. The engineers at IBM were having trouble with noise on telephone lines used to transmit information between computers. While studying the problem, Mandelbrot learned that the traditional method of thinking had caused the IBM engineers to ignore certain information in their analysis. Once this piece of information was discovered, he was able to begin to fashion a solution to the problem. He realized that there was never a time during which the errors were scattered continuously, but that they came in bursts. This observation led to a consistent relationship between the bursts of errors and the spaces of clean transmission. This highly abstract description for a practical problem had significant consequences for scientists trying to decide between different theories for controlling error. In the past when the engineers had tried to explain the errors, they always looked for a man sticking a screwdriver someplace he should not. Mandelbrot understood that they would never understand the source of the errors by looking at local occurrences. He began to draw on other streams of data, including information about the height of the Nile River in Egypt, to explain this phenomenon. As a result of this data and his study of discontinuities within this and other streams of data, he began an organized study of the phenomena. On a wintry afternoon in 1975 while preparing a major work for publication in book form, he decided on a name for the shapes he had discovered while analyzing these data streams. The images created where graphic representations of the complexity of chaos and the order hidden within. Mandelbrot called these shapes, "fractals." The Mandelbrot sets represent some of the most beautiful and compelling images created by any science.

No matter how complex the data stream, patterns will emerge from the disorder. The following are examples of Mandelbrot and Julia sets. Julia sets were invented in studies during World War I by Gaston Julia and Pierre Fatou. They were drawn without the aide of a computer. Mandelbrot later enhanced these sets using an iterative process and modern computers.

First the Mandelbrot sets.

Mandelbrot Set: Lode with two branches

.

Mandelbrot Set:Lobe with three branches

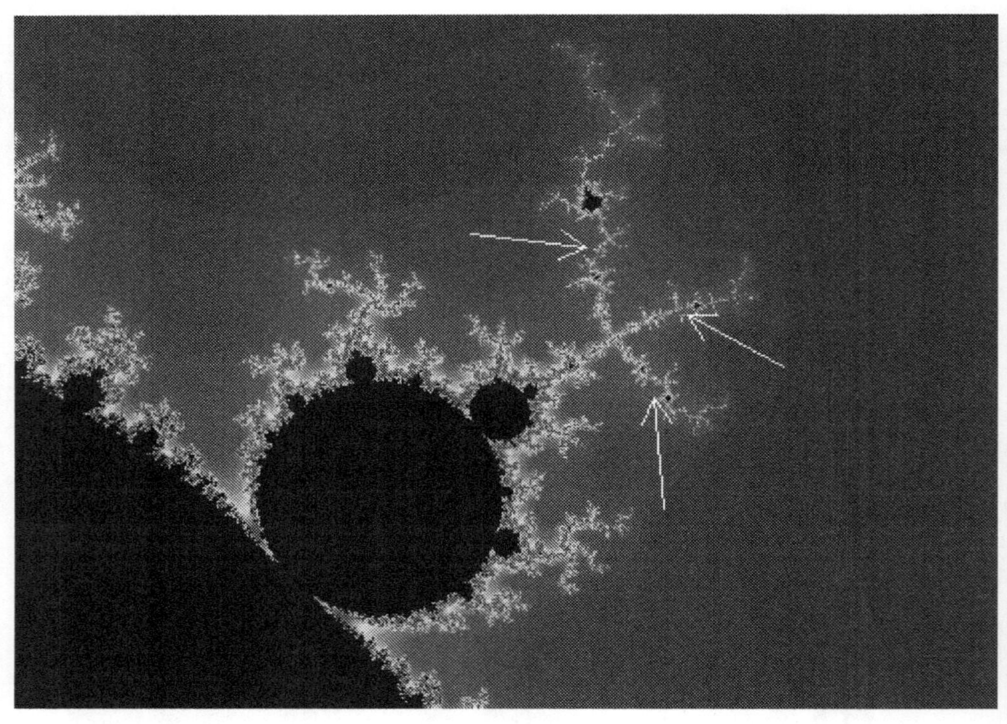

.

Mandelbrot Set: Lobe with four Branches

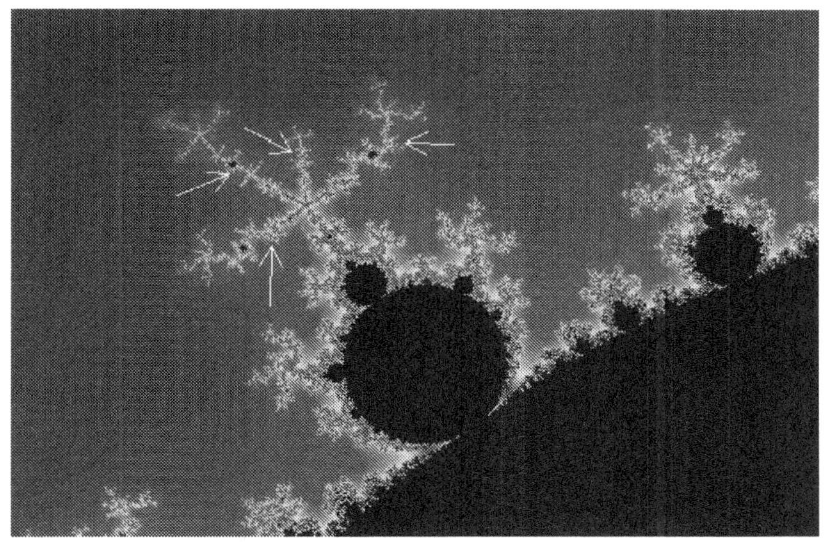

Julia Set 1

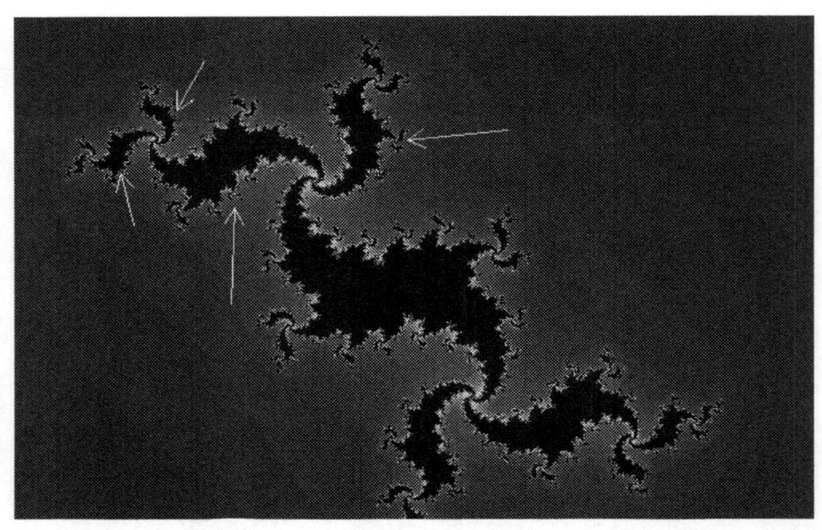

Julia Set 2

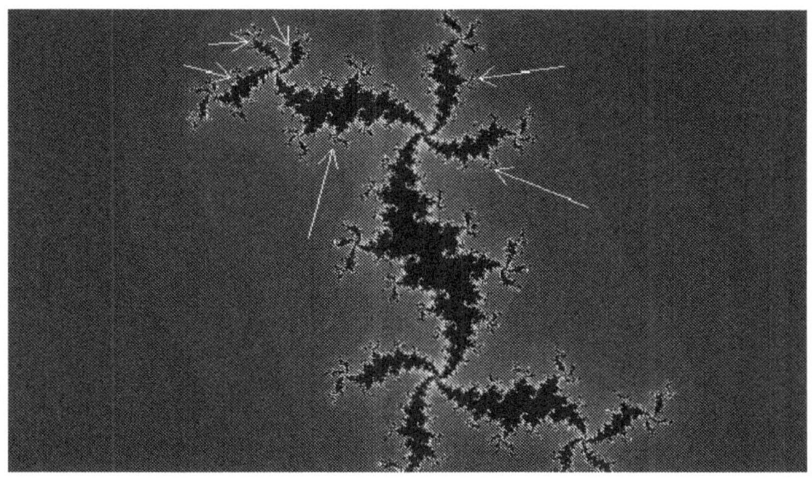

Julia Set 3

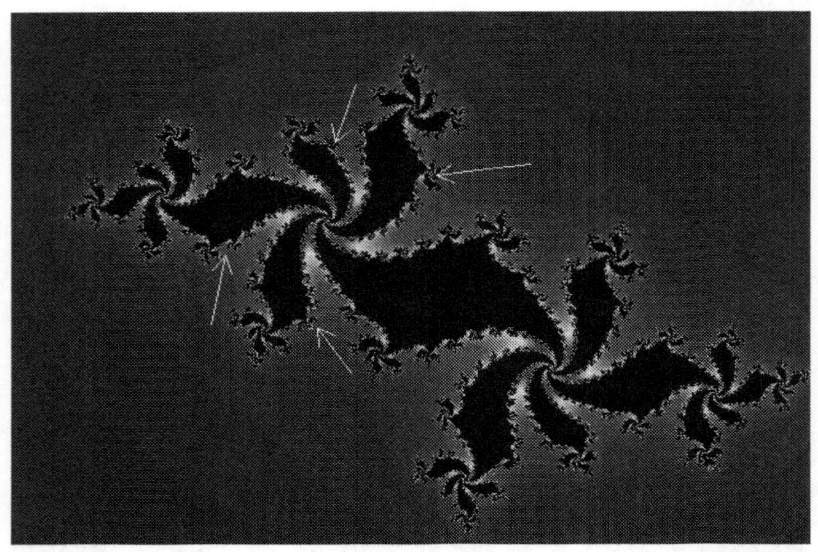

Illustrations from-- http://learn.sdstate.edu/cogswelk/ChaosFractals/Chapter_7_MORE_FRACTALS/Mandlebrot/Mandlebrot.htm, 2005

Chaos theory helps us understand that even in the most complex disorder with staggering numbers of variables, we can find patterns of activity or regularities in the chaos, which can form themselves into systems. This is the very thing that we can see as we study the early farming communities of the Fertile Crescent. The farming communities established recurrent patterns of activity around the cultivation of plants and domestication of animals. These are not the only variables in place at the time, but they are two of the most significant. They point the way to the establishment of property ownership of cultivated plants and domesticated animals and the formation of patterns in the complex and chaotic activity of pre-history.

It was just this type of approach that I was looking for in my analysis of activity in the Fertile Crescent at the start of human farming. Chaos theory is a useful tool to understand the complex and regular patterns of human behavior during this critical time.

A fresh reading of the book *Sync* quickly led me to discussions of the work of Stephen Smale and finally Robert M. May. Each had completed work on the study of population systems, asking and seeking such answers as to how populations of certain species behaved with limited food supplies or with the addition of predators to the population. These were the types of questions in which I had an interest for during the period in which farming started. May had carried out a numerical analysis into the behavior of populations using simple sets of equations. Although these equations may appear simple to mathematicians, to those of us who are not, they can be daunting. Nonetheless, I waded into the reading of these works, looking for some clue that might lead me to understand what was happening with human populations in the Fertile Crescent. Slowly, and sometimes quite painfully, I began to understand some of the principles of these works.

The model used by May in his study of populations moved between steady state and oscillation with certain changes in parameters. He understood that complex communities were inherently more stable than simple ones. May was the first to ask what would happen if the systems received a sudden large input, or kick, the kind of thing that would happen when there is a significant change introduced to a population's environment. In this case, he was talking about the introduction of such things as immunizations when considering epidemics. What he found was that huge oscillations occurred in the mathematical model which create radical shifts in the populations themselves. He backed up this theory with data obtained from doctors in Britain in a campaign to wipe out rubella. The introduction of the serum to combat the disease produced the same type of population oscillations. These oscillations he surmised were patterns of order emerging. The system would adjust and reach a new point of equilibrium despite the complexity.

The introduction of farming to hunter-gatherer societies was just such a huge input to human groups in the Fertile Crescent. As described by May, its introduction would result in oscillations (instability) occurring that will eventually settle into a stable system. Animal populations tended to decline from hunting during this time while wild grains proliferated. Choosing these plants as a food source would provide a larger and more stable food supply. This would be a substantial new input, or kick, to human populations.

The way natural systems adapt to a significant input has been seen in real-world examples such as wildlife populations in Canada studied over a timeframe exceeding 200 years. The populations would respond to various kicks to the system, resulting in a new equilibrium associated with peaks in population. So, despite the apparent chaotic nature of these complex relationships, patterns begin to emerge. These sudden, large inputs resulted in oscillations, or flurries, of new activity as the populations worked to assimilate the new input. In the case of human populations in the Fertile Crescent, this new input was the resultant stable food supply and changing requirements from foraging to sedimentary behavior by humans to protect and maintain that food source.

At this point, we can begin to see the emergence of some type of pattern in the oscillations of populations as they try to assimilate certain kicks to the system. This leads us directly to the question of how such oscillations behave. Steven Strogatz, in his publication *Sync: The Emerging Science of Spontaneous Order* published by Theia Press, 2003, moves the process forward to understand how the behavior of these oscillations can result in interconnectedness. In his book, there are discussions of studies of populations of certain species, in particular, a discussion of studies of large groups of fireflies seen in western Asia. Oddly enough, these groups of insects exhibit a unique characteristic which has been observed by scholars for over 300 years. At times, enormous congregations of the fireflies will collect and will blink on and off in unison, a type of synchronous behavior. As the fireflies gathered, they reach a critical mass, which results in synchronous behavior. There is a large kick to the population that resulted in synchronous activity, just as discussed in the case of population models used by May. The kick here occurs as the population reaches a certain limit. When this happens, the behavior of the overall population changes significantly. The synchronous activity develops around a certain density of the group and certain rhythms of blinking.

This behavior has been seen in mechanical systems as well. For engineers, it is a well-known phenomenon that banks of oscillators operating in close proximity to each other will exhibit the same synchronous behavior. The oscillators will begin to operate in a synchronous pattern with each. But whether looking at biological activity or at mechanical activity, the driving forces tend to be the same: there is some type of massive kick to the system, or build up of forces; a type of pressure increase occurs and when it reaches a threshold, the population moves to spread the pressure to other members within the population and the result is a benefit to the whole population as it moves toward stability, or synchronous behavior. Phillip Laurent, John Buck, and Hugh Smith are among the many scholars that have documented this behavior.

For the first time, we can see how the introduction of a significant new input, or kick, to a population, in our case farming, would move human populations to a sort of oscillatory behavior and to seek a new level of equilibrium. This process will start as a natural phenomena and proceed to organize itself around three principles: surplus, a need to distribute it in some manner of exchange, and the resultant benefit to the group of stability. These three recognized principles are also typical of self-organizing behavior, or synchronicity, in general.

We can begin to see these self-organizing principles take hold and adopt human behavior accordingly. In order to accommodate this new kick to the system of farming, the populations work to assimilate the new input and, as a result, begin to distribute to other members of the group in order to receive the benefit of stability, or equilibrium. A simple concise concept is in place. It is not a human system but a natural one of which humans are a part. This brings us to the question of the impact caused by farming. What was it?

Surplus

The interesting concept of shocks, or kicks, to the system is intriguing. Although there had been considerable discussion of this phenomenon as we talked about oscillators and groups of insects, how exactly did it apply to groups of human beings in the dawn of history? My readings indicated that there were several parallels in modern human studies concerning menstrual periods in women who worked or lived in close proximity to each other for long periods of time, yet there was nothing to make a direct connection between these studies and human populations in the Fertile Crescent. In the middle of my ruminations, I found a passage in Ehrenberg's work that makes this connection. Along with developing tools and techniques for simple horticulture farming would come the development of skills to create some types of permanent structures in the area where the grain was being cultivated. Likewise would have followed the development of structures for storing and containing the grains. Ehrenberg references the excavation of a site at Mureybet dating from about 10000 to 8000 B.C.E. where there were quite substantial rectangular huts built which contain storage bins in the floors of the houses. The walls of these houses had been plastered repeatedly, indicating an unusual degree of permanence. Ehrenberg next postulates:

> *As people became committed to living more or less permanently in one location because of the*

> *agricultural cycle, and began to build places to store things, they would have found it easier to accumulate possessions, such as ornaments, storage containers, and tools. . .*
>
> *. . . Another consequence of the ability to keep material possessions and to store food was for the first time some people could accumulate more than others. If someone needed a tool or emergency supply of food that someone else had in surplus it could be borrowed or accepted as a gift, and the borrower would become indebted to the lender or giver. So wealth, debt and obligation, and hence social stratification based on a differential ownership, could have begun to develop for the first time in the Neolithic Period.* (Ehrenberg, 1989)

There is also considerable discussion about how this creation of surplus would have affected the population density. For the first time, women would be able to have multiple children because the permanence of the early farming settlements would allow for enough food and stability to care for these numbers. In a forging society always on the move, a woman can care for one child, but it is impossible to care for more than one. Farming and its resultant stability would mean a significant increase in population growth built around the concept of surplus food. It was this concept of surplus which acted as a giant kick to the population of humans in this area to move them forward in the evolutionary fashion.

As the system began to self-organize or become synchronous, groups of fledgling farmers would have developed methods to store grain as well as methods to grow it. Having already made the step to begin domesticating certain animals which would have frequented the same regions in search of food and cultivating the grains being grown in these areas, these groups would find themselves with a surplus of a critical commodity: food. As we have seen with other groups and systems, this sudden kick to the system causes it to seek a new equilibrium and will result in many cases in synchronous behavior. In the case of farming, humans would begin to engage in trade around the surplus foodstuffs they were now able to accumulate. This synchronous activity would continue as long as the foodstuffs could be obtained in quantity. Synchronous activity would create a stable community and began the first steps toward trading within the community. Three things have now occurred: we have surplus, which is a significant kick to the system; we have the system seeking to adjust to this new input by distributing the input to other members of the group in some fashion, i.e. exchange or trade; finally, we have the resultant benefit to the group of a new type of stability as it absorbs this new input: a type of profit. Surplus, markets, and profits are the three tenants that define the natural system of Capitalism as it has evolved with and shaped human behavior.

As we have seen throughout this discussion, the system began its evolution in recurring patterns of activity. From the chaotic mix of human activity, a type of order began to evolve, which ultimately became self-organizing, or synchronous. The system that was created had a significant impact on human behavior; it moved early humans from foragers to settlers. The affected population grew by allowing mothers the time and resources to be able to care for multiple offspring. There would have been a resultant decrease, albeit small, in infant mortality because of these changes. Being in a fixed area for longer periods of time would have allowed for the creation of sturdy and stable structures, including storage facilities for excess grain and food. Once there was accumulated surplus in the nature of foodstuffs, the system imposed more changes on the group by encouraging trade to redistribute this surplus on an as-needed basis to group members in exchange for other needed items: profit. The system was altering human behavior in fundamental ways.

There are still some outstanding questions to be answered. In particular, what was so unique about this particular group of humans and their relationship with farming? After all, there are groups of nomads that display tendencies toward permanence by staying in one area over a long period of time. We see such examples in societies in Palestine, coastal Peru, and Japan.

Likewise, there are groups of horticulture farming societies which are mobile. Examples of these would be the peoples of New Guinea and American Indian tribes of the Southwest. In truth, there is no hard and fast distinction between these types and our prototypical farmer. Jared Diamond, in his book *Guns, Germs, and Steel: The Fates of Human Societies*, discusses some of these questions in detail. Although his book deals in great detail with many other areas of the world, he does discuss the growth of farming in the Fertile Crescent and its resultant spread to Europe. The surplus created in these fledgling communities was the key to the head start Europe would have on the rest of the world in cultural development. He arrives at his conclusions based upon a study of cultures. I, on the other hand, am approaching it from the viewpoint of a natural system, Capitalism. We agree in one fundamental concept: there was no creation or invention of farming or food production. Before this, human beings had no concept of farming. They were simple hunter-gatherer's who adopted their behavior in response to the formation of a natural system. As Jared Diamond points out in his book,

> *... the first people who adopted food production, obviously could not have been making a conscious choice or consciously striving toward farming as a goal because they had never seen farming and had no way of knowing what it would be like ...* (Diamond, 2000)

This system was the beginning of Capitalism in the agricultural context. We find additional support for this position in the work of Ellen Meiksins Wood, *The Agrarian Origins of Capitalism*. The natural system of Capitalism formed around surplus food stores and began in farming communities. These communities would not be the only communities in existence at the time. The evolution of the natural system would have taken many generations and hundreds, if not thousands, of years. During this time, there would still be hunter-gatherer societies in existence. There would be other types of farming enclaves that would come into existence as well. The important concept is the difference between Capitalism and these other systems. This difference is the reason that Capitalism has spread so prolifically throughout the world. Capitalism is not only self-organizing, it is capable of replicating itself.

MEMES

When we talk about living systems, use of the term "self-replicating" is easily understood. In the instance of natural systems, drawing a parallel with biological systems is fraught with dangers. Yet, for any natural system to succeed and continue, there must be some type of replication. This principle was first put together by Richard Dawkins in his book *The Selfish Gene*, in which Dawkins discusses how certain concepts could be transmitted throughout cultures. In biological systems, it is readily accepted that traits are transmitted by genes. He postulated that there is a gene equivalent associated with cultural transmission which he turned into the "meme."

There are numerous examples of how memes transmit themselves in culture. We've all heard songs which seemed to be infectious, passing quite quickly from person to person. Likewise, we have seen advertisements and ideas that moved through the culture in the same fashion. In his book, Dawkins relates a most interesting story about a bird called the saddleback in an island off the coast of New Zealand. This same story was recounted by Steven Strogatz in his book *Sync: The Emerging Science of Spontaneous Behavior*. Apparently, these birds communicate by transmission of a group of songs. Each new generation is taught these songs by prior generations. Sometimes, a particular song will not be repeated exactly, but will undergo modification either through a mistake or by intentional design. This is an example of non-genetic transmission. Memes then, are the cultural equivalent of genes and are used to replicate and propagate ideas. This is the way that good ideas move from culture to culture. But, just as there is competition within the gene pool between different species, so is there competition in the cultural soup between ideas or memes. Good ideas are imitated and bad ideas fall to the wayside in much the same way as do defective gene patterns.

Not all ideas will be able to undergo this replication and continue their existence. Dawkins establishes parameters for the successful transmission and replication of an idea, or memes: copying fidelity (the number of times it has been successfully exchanged or can be successfully exchanged with others), fecundity, and longevity. These items strangely mirror the three pillars of Capitalism: surplus, exchange, and benefit/profit. The most successful ideas will compete in a vigorous manner to displace other ideas in the cultural pool. Although we cannot attach human traits such as viciousness or ruthlessness, there is significant and severe competition within the cultural broth for survival. Capitalism is ideally suited for repetition. As an idea, or meme, it is easily reproducible and will tolerate a great deal of flexibility in reproduction. That is you don't have to reproduce the model exactly for it to proliferate, like coping fidelity. Capitalism requires an exchange as well, comparable to fecundity. Finally, Capitalism is long-lived, as required in longevity of memes. Capitalism is not ruthless, but it is a very vigorous system that is well-suited for survival in human culture. As the natural system has progressed, it has been favored in the cultural soup by being imitated, the primary form of replication for ideas, or memes. When you began to think of Capitalism, you should not think of a flower but of a weed. Capitalism is a hearty system which can survive better than most the calamities and pitfalls which can create instability and resultant destruction of a natural system. Capitalism is constantly evolving. Each stage of evolution has created resultant changes in human behavior.

When I started looking for answers as to what Capitalism was and where it came from, I did not expect to find the answers that I did. The development of chaos theory and synchronicity have allowed us to see the creation of this concept, this natural system, in a very different way. By following its meager beginnings in the Fertile Crescent, we can see how a specific group of people would be moved along by the evolution of this natural system toward Capitalism. We can likewise see how the system might have transmitted itself in an attempt at cultural survival. However, the process does not stop here. A single cluster of humans being embraced by this system does not explain how the system has spread so prolifically. We now have basic components of the system and a means of spread, but we must look further to explain its overall survival. After all, the farming community is a long way from a nation.

Farming Villages to Towns and Cities

Agrarian Capitalism, farming, would go on to spread through the Fertile Crescent and into Europe. As we can see from the illustration below, farming would expand into parts of Asia over the next several thousand years. The spectacular proliferation occurred because memes had basic survival characteristics which Dawkins described as an easily imitated system not requiring exact replication to be successful that has longevity. The surpluses created by the system made it possible for certain other technological innovations to occur. It created time to consider new farming techniques, building techniques, and establishing certain social structures once the overwhelming need to continuously search for food was removed. Families could grow larger because of the stability created by the system. This would consequently results in population growth. More importantly, it would result in social stratification.

Not every farming group, or agrarian capitalist node, would be successful. Some would fail because of poor skills, bad soil conditions, the capriciousness of nature, or through the intervention of other groups of humans in conflict. Whatever the reason, some of the farming groups would need to obtain food sources from the more successful groups. This would be a continuation of the social stratification we had discussed internally within the groups. There would become haves and have-nots. Those that had successful surpluses would be able to dictate terms and conditions of those seeking to obtain it. These less fortunate individuals might in some cases become members of successful groups or simply begin to engage in trade for food or other items. This social stratification associated with agricultural Capitalism would continue as the system continued to evolve.

The connections beginning to form between the individual groups would also be important in another way. Individual groups would begin to exchange product between those that were in close physical proximity. As more and more connections were made between groups, this interconnectivity would have introduced a new kick to the system.

The Spread of Farming

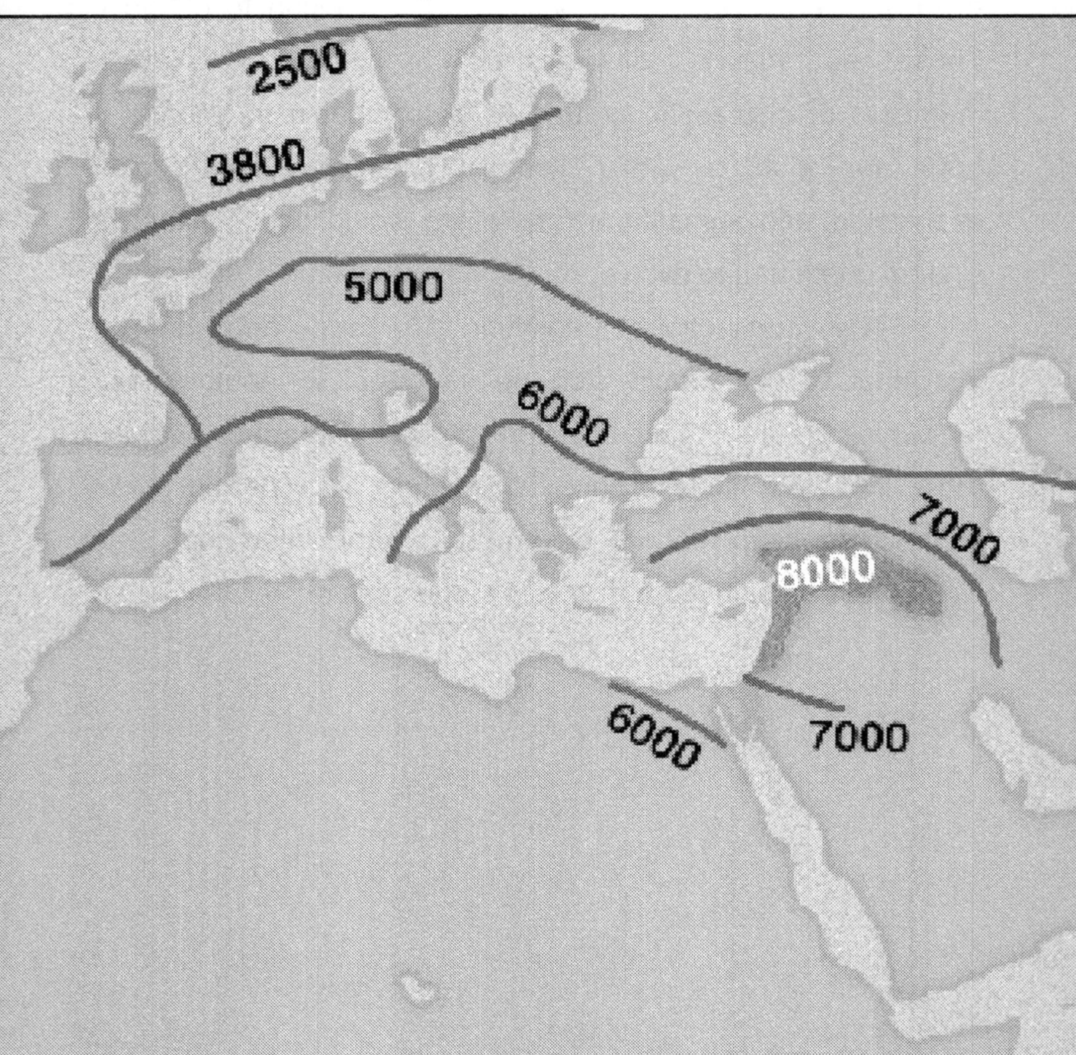

http://www.unl.edu/rhames/courses/orig_agri_tur.html, from the Jared Diamond web site

The Spread of Food Production from the Fertile Crescent.

The dark-shaded area is the Crescent itself, where food production was established by 8000 B.C.E. Lines denote how far food production, on the basis mostly of Fertile Crescent crops and livestock, had spread by the indicated dates.

The richness of the connections between the groups would transport not only product but cultural change and innovation. The influences being transmitted through contact with other groups would create a sort of system sensitivity. This was first described by Arthur Winfrey in his "Biological Rhythms and the Behavior of Populations of Couple Oscillators," published in *Journal of Theoretical Biology 16* (1967), pages15-42. According to Winfrey's theory, there would be a sort of incoherence or new chaos set up among the groups. The system would struggle to create a new equilibrium, or stability. It would try to spontaneously organize into synchronous behavior. The success of this effort would depend on the makeup of the individual nodes, or groups forming interconnections. Some would be compatible and some not. Two groups would form: those through which trade could occur and those that offered no promise of further trade. The connection between like nodes or groups would increase, as connections between dissimilar or rejected groups would decrease and ultimately stop. As these favorable interconnections and contacts increased, there would be a sort of synchronization between the groups beginning to occur. They would begin collapsing into a larger system as many new connections would form in the new chaos. This would be caused by increased trade established between the groups, spurred on by different types of surplus and different types of technological developments within each group.

As these connections increase, we reached a critical threshold. This threshold, known as a tipping point, has been described in a number of applications from oscillators to social groups. When the interconnections reach a critical threshold, they begin to accelerate the rapid formation of new connections. At or near the threshold point, the connections began to represent a significant change, or kick to the system, just as we saw with the introduction of farming to the initial groups. However, in this case, it is the interconnections and transfer of cultural ideas between the groups which creates a new system as groups begin to collapse into a network. The speed-up in interconnectedness will continue until a certain density is obtained. At this time, a new tipping point is reached and the number of interconnections between the groups, or nodes, will began to drop off and stop. This will occur because the amount of change being introduced by new or subsequent interconnections will represent an almost negligible impact on the system at this time. The interconnections between the groups will have become so numerous that no single connection represents significant new input. The system then begins to stabilize around this larger network. In describing the way natural systems work in synchronous behavior, we can begin to see, independent of biology or physics, how towns and cities would begin to form all round the initial groups. This clustering effect brought on by interconnections would be the method for transmitting cultural ideas that would take root over the next several thousand years, as cities began to form themselves from localized farming groups.

It is clear that farming spread from the Fertile Crescent throughout much of Europe and Asia. It is likewise well-established that farming communities existed in other parts of the world. However, it was European civilization which made the greatest strides in technology and social order. As Jared Diamond points out in his book *Guns, Germs and Steel*, this was largely due to the availability of surplus, which would give Europeans time and leisure to pursue technologies, philosophies, and science. Diamond explained the reason for the surplus as a fortuitous location in a friendly Mediterranean region, populated by favorable plants and animals in abundance. Whatever the reason for the surplus, it spurred the evolution of agricultural Capitalism in these small groups. They moved from farming communities into centers of human activity first as cities, and then as states and countries, by this clustering effect, in the same way that other models did, going from chaos to synchronous behavior. In a very real sense, it was the natural system of Capitalism which was imposing changes and order on human society in very subtle ways as the system worked to assimilate inputs and to create stability. These changes ultimately would lead to an explosion of cultural richness that would move western culture far ahead of many of the other regions of the world.

From relatively meager beginnings in 8500 B.C.E., Capitalism would settle into a relatively stable period of expansion and contraction until after the birth of Christ. The system would see many changes during that period of time in the form of wars, climate change, epidemics, and the rise of other systems such as philosophy, politics, and the beginnings of science. The system would not remain at a fixed size but would contract and expand with population increases and decreases. Depending upon the state of hostilities between regions, a particular connection might be severed for a short period of time only to be renewed once hostilities had ceased. This flexibility in the system of Capitalism allowed it to stay in place and intact throughout much of human cultural development. As cities became states and regions controlled by philosophies and politics, the underlying driving force for stability was always the system of Capitalism with its simple three-pronged message: create surplus, engage in exchange, and achieve some type of benefit or profit. Whether we are talking about the creation of kingdoms or of individual groups in the Fertile Crescent, the underlying principle will remain the same. The cultural meme of Capitalism, with its flexibility and tenacity, continued to survive and to shape Western culture fundamentally. Looking at the time frame beginning at around 2000 B.C.E., we begin to see the rise of the first great civilizations built around the same three principles: surplus, markets, and profits. But, the complex system which had evolved was limited in one key area: production of surplus.

As a system, Capitalism expanded and reorganized itself from periods of chaos to synchronous order to a more broad-scale system involving cities and states in the Western world as trade occurred largely on a regional basis. However, this trade was small in proportion to populations. In Europe, countries in close proximity would engage in trade across regional boundaries, which was often limited by production and ability to transport. Ships would carry a certain quantity of cargo to ports only when such cargo was available. By and large, until we reach the beginning of the 14th or 15th century, ships, barges, and other waterborne transportation systems are the most economical method of transporting quantities of goods, but they operated at the mercy of the forces of nature. By contrast, transportation of goods overland was limited to animal borne transportation. In both cases, the amount of material that could be transported was small and of a limited type. Consequently, the system that had come into being was largely stable because it was limited by means of production and transportation. You might be able to buy English merchandise in Paris to a limited degree or buy samples of Chinese silks and pottery in England to an equally limited degree, but quantities of trade goods would become available to the common population only when there was a change in the methods of production and transportation.

An interesting observation about the early stages of Europe and its association with Capitalism concerns the relative stability of the system. For example, in Europe, as it evolved from agricultural farming communities into tribes and kingdoms, changes were easily accommodated by Capitalism. The communities, tribes, and kingdoms within Europe tended to be of a relative uniform size when looking at the surplus they produced. A sensitivity had develop within the natural system: the size of the individual nodes. Some sense of uniformity is required in order for the system to function smoothly. As Europe settled into a long period of stable and synchronous activity around agricultural surplus, this relative uniformity in node size was an important factor. As communities and cities began to form, trade would continue. As the communities and cities operated in this system, no one specific node represented a disproportionate input of surplus to this system. Most of the trading activity was centered in and around Europe and its neighboring countries with very little global trade. The occasional ships or caravans to the Americas and the Far East represented a relatively minor input to the system in terms of trade goods. Until we reach the 1700s, the system of

Capitalism was operating very stably. The colonies of the Americas were operating as extensions of their European masters, and until the 1700s, were in the same situation as Russia. While representing large land masses, their input to the system of surplus goods was small. However, with so many things that happen in life, timing is everything. This change occurred just at the time that political systems within Europe were least likely to recognize them and their importance to the stability of the system which had served them so well, for so long: Capitalism.

The stability of the system was to receive another huge kick as we moved into the 16th and 17th centuries: industrialization. Until this time, technologies had largely been used to enhance the quality of goods and services rather than increase quantity. The craftsman and his ability to produce were still the limiting factors for quantities of goods. With industrialization, we move away from the limits of the human component and into a time when mechanical systems were able to create huge quantities of surplus and provide the reliable transportation systems necessary to move that surplus throughout the system. As we've seen in the past, such a shock to the system will create instability until the connections have been worked out sufficiently to allow for distribution throughout the network. Such distribution was not to be allowed at the beginning of industrialization because of the limits imposed by emerging political systems the time.

Government vs. Capitalism

Capitalism settled into a graceful, stable, and easy existence alongside human cultures as it expanded from the Fertile Crescent throughout Europe and other parts of the globe. The symbiotic relationship between farming and its creation of surplus and Capitalism was working well for humanity. Between 8500 B.C.E. and 5500 B.C.E., human cultures had evolved from simple farming communities into primitive chiefdoms with the very rudimentary beginnings of a political structure. These early social organizations, which were often composed of some type of leadership council or a single leader, would direct activities for the entire group. Political systems were not the only systems to begin evolution at this time. There were also the evolution of philosophies, or religions, in an effort to explain man's place in a larger universe. However, it is the social system of governments which is most important because of its severe impact on Capitalism. Politics would evolve from crude control over rough geographical areas into a more sophisticated system of control as humans groups were transformed from farming communities into cities.

The overall function of government is to provide controls and restrictions on human behavior. These restrictions can sometimes take the form of religions dicta and in others, the form of codes governing behavior such as was used by Hammerabi in the first written code of behavior for human societies. Whatever the source, the end result was to move human societies into a more controlled and regulated activity: government. The next table shows the development of some of these systems.

Eurasian Development

	Fertile Crescent	China	England
Plant Domestication	8500 B.C.	by 7500 B.C.	3500 B.C.
Animal Domestication	8000 B.C.	by 7500 B.C.	3500 B.C.
Pottery	7000 B.C.	by 7500 B.C.	3500 B.C.
Villages	9000 B.C.	By 7500 B.C.	3000 B.C.
Chiefdoms	5500 B.C.	4000 B.C.	2500 B.C.
States	3700 B.C.	2000 B. C.	500 A.D.
Writing	3200 B.C.	by 1300 B.C.	43 A.D.
Metal Tools	900 B.C.	500 B.C.	650 B.C.

Partial reconstruction of Jared Diamond's table 18.1 from, "*Guns, Germs and Steel*"

This table gives approximate dates of significant developments toward the development of modern nation-building in Eurasia. (We note that the domestication of dogs occurred far earlier than shown.)

Humanities involvement with empires would result in the creation of laws to not only control and direct human behavior, but what humans could do with their assets: their surplus. It was inevitable that human culture in the form of government systems would soon begin to compete with Capitalism for control of the very factors which made the system function. The competition would start in truth when farming created the first surplus, and the first group of neophyte farmers moved to protect it as their food supply. It would take many thousands of years before these concepts would become organized and eventually ingrained into the fabric of human society.

I am being careful here to draw a distinction between society and culture. Culture encompasses a much broader spectrum of human behavior; society deals with the more modern concept of governance and its relation to social systems. So it was that as human cultures evolved, society came into creation and began to have a significant impact upon the way human culture functioned. Key concepts would be developed dealing with property and contract that would impact not only social systems but have a tremendous impact upon the natural system: Capitalism.

From the moment the first farmer created surplus and made an agreement to trade a portion of the surplus to another human being, humanity became involved with the concept of contract. In Europe and Eurasia, this concept would develop over several thousand years dating from 2500 B.C.E. until 1500 C.E. For many thousands of years, the surplus belonged jointly to the person who created it and to the forces, armies, kingdoms, or individuals who could exert enough force to command a portion of it as their own. Very often this was a king, tribal chieftain, or local entity with the military capacity to command payment. The relationship between the farmers who created the surplus and these political entities would first become identified in a type of arrangement for protection, and later on, become more formalized into a contractual relationship between the individuals and the state. “Contract,” as it would become known in modern times, dealt with society's need to handle the creation of debt. Parties were often involved in transactions in which one would promise to do something or place a portion of their personal assets as security for something. The formalization of this relationship into written and verbal documents defined how all goods and services would be transferred between individuals or entities: contract. In the latter part of the 12th century C.E. with the creation of court systems, the concept of contract would act as a control mechanism on the transfer of property and goods between individuals. Whereas Capitalism had worked in a natural exchange of surplus between those that had it and those that needed it, society was changing the rules of the game. Now these exchanges of goods, property, and material would be governed by social constructs and not by the natural system. This brings us to an important concept: property.

Surplus, as we saw in the early stages of Capitalism, dealt with the creation of additional material, foodstuffs, clothing, tools, or services that could be utilized by the larger group. As society came into existence with governments and courts, the definition of property came into being as well. An individual no longer had to defend what they created by force of arms; the force of law now dictated what property the individual owned and protected it. Just as in Rome, highways were built for the public and protected by Roman legions, so, too, in the modern world, property as a concept was created and fostered by governments in much the same way. Determining who owned property was much easier when the government defined the term property so that there was a uniform definition for all parties which made it easier for governments to tax the property. The creation of property rights and contracts put into place a concept that would force society to create restraints on the flow of goods. Governments justified this restriction on the basis of taxation. After all, taxes would be used to pay for improvements for the common man.

The forces of government organized rapidly throughout much of Europe. By the time we reach the 15th and 16th century, radical reformation of the agricultural farming system was under way. The concept of contract and property were defined in terms of taxes and wealth. Three developments would come together in time to create the phenomena that we recognize as the Industrial Revolution. It is this synchronicity of these events that moved Capitalism from a system being driven by surplus into one being driven by profit.

The first of those events was the application of the " Inclosure Acts" throughout much of England, resulting in a dramatic increase in agricultural production. The second event was the change in methods of production with the advent of the steam engine and mechanization. The final item was not a great surprise, but as we have seen so often in nature, the luck of the draw. England, a country of relatively small population and geographical area, was located on huge natural deposits of coal. The occurrence in time, or the synchronous happening of these three items, would spark the Industrial Revolution.

Prior to the 15th and 16th century, much of farming throughout Europe consisted of individuals using large open fields which were common in many areas of the country. These common areas were available for the public or to rent and were usually associated with medieval manors. Farming families or groups could use these areas of land for production. As early as the 12th century in England, many of these fields and common areas were being broken up and converted to private ownership. The result was a displacement of large numbers of the population from the land and into urban areas, or cities. The first wave of "Inclosure Acts" affected mostly Central England where this land was converted to pasturing sheep for wool production. Open farmland had been commonly used as pasture land for sheep from the 14th to the 16th century, but the increase in demand for wool encouraged many English lords to use the common areas for the production of wool.

Feudal holdings were an ideal place for such an endeavor. Large areas of land around the feudal estate were maintained in common areas and could be readily utilized for the pasturing of sheep. Wool prices made this particularly attractive and cost-effective since the land did not have to be purchased. As a common area, it was available for anyone to use. Over time, the usage of the land had been restricted to those who had permission from the feudal lord for its use. This worked well for the holders of the estates because now they could exert control over large areas of land for the production of wool. However, this became very problematic for the emerging central government in England. The process of sheep herding was far less manpower-intensive than family farming. Many family farming groups were being displaced from the land by the new enterprise. Homes that once housed families working land in the common areas soon fell into disrepair and became unsuitable for habitation of any type. This process forced larger numbers of families from the common areas and into the cities where they would seek housing and employment. In rural areas controlled largely by the remnants of feudalism, the Lords, the movement of the people from the common areas was desirable; for the emerging central government who had to provide services and jobs for these people in the urban centers, it was not. Yet even if these people wanted to move back to the common areas, the deterioration of many of the homes made it impossible.

The central government was left with a dilemma of rising populations within the cities and a declining tax base. The solution to this problem was simple: increase the tax base. However, in an agrarian society, it is often not easy to create jobs for an unskilled labor force. This set up a classic conflict between the central government and the Lords over the control of land. The result was the central government passed a series of acts designed to break up the common areas and to pass them into private ownership. This allowed the central government to tax the land and the enterprises conducted on the land to raise revenue for the government. While sound in theory, the implementation of this process did not work as expected. As the common areas were broken up and placed in private ownership, some of it was indeed returned to farming but with greatly reduced numbers of farmers. Family farming was simply too inefficient for the needs of modern entrepreneurs who wanted profit rather than stable families. The smaller and more efficient farms created were highly profitable for the owners and for the government. It was only a matter of time before many of the existing estates were broken up and sold into private ownership. This resulted in the destruction of the last vestiges of power for feudalism and the establishment of a strong central government within England. It also set the framework for a more efficient model of farming based upon smaller numbers of people being used more efficiently. Finally, the Inclosure Consolidation Act of 1801 removed the last of the common areas from feudal estates and placed them into private ownership.

The intent of these acts had been to address the needs of large numbers of people being dislocated from the rural countryside and moving into the cities. This unintended consequence was to accelerate this process and to create large numbers of unemployed people within the urban centers as a ready source of cheap labor. While establishing private ownership of property, which would become the bedrock of Western legal systems, this process also established firmly the dominance of the central government in England as the force in that country. The establishment of a strong central government became ingrained in the social fabric of England with the printing of Adam Smith's *Wealth of Nations* in 1776. The establishment of this theory and the existence of cheap labor pools were only one part of what was needed to spark the Industrial Revolution.

The second part of the equation was to be technology. England had the good fortune to be located over vast quantities of coal. In order to access this material used for heating and manufacturing, mining was necessary. The process of extraction is a labor-intensive endeavor. In order to reduce the costs of excessive labor, mining interest were quick to seize upon a new technological development to be used in the coal mines, a new engine which would allow for mechanization and reduce the need for laborers. This new technology was eagerly applied only to find that it had an Achilles' heel: the earliest mechanisms tended to be reliable for only a short period of time because the steam chamber would begin to cool and the engine stopped operating once it dropped below a certain temperature. Mining interests struggled with the new technology for several years until an assistant engineer by the name of James Watt solved the problems of the steam cycle. With his innovation, there was now a steam engine that could run for 24 hours a day extracting coal from the mines. This new device, although first used within coal mines, soon found other applications in manufacturing. The textile industries, leather industries, and a number of other industries soon found applications for this new technology. With a stable engine, abundant coal, and cities teeming with unemployed workers, all the elements for the Industrial Revolution were in place. Soon, manufacturing would be fully under way.

This prompted a massive surge in surplus being produced by English manufacturers. It also spurred the development of other technologies by enterprising individuals seeking to make profit from technological innovation. As other countries around Europe saw developments within England and the massive quantities of new products and new technologies being developed, they raced to catch up. Soon throughout Europe, technological innovation was in full bloom.

A system that had been stable for thousands of years was now being forced to undergo rapid change. What had taken thousands of years in the past would now happen within a matter of decades. As products and new technologies began to abound, so, too, did the exchange of information between countries and groups become more prolific. New interconnections were being established to accommodate the new inputs into this system. Interconnections are the way that memes transmit desirable characteristics and cultural information as well as technological information throughout the system. It is the central way of keeping the system stable. With more technological innovation, there was more information, products, and technology to be redistributed for system stability. Capitalism was adjusting to a new input, or in this case, many new inputs being spurred by technological innovation. Now, the difference was that surplus was no longer the driving force for the system; it was profit. Surplus was being generated in terms of goods, technology, and innovation to increase profits. Yet, it does not matter what causes the input, the system reacts in the same way: it struggles to redistribute the excess to keep the system stable. This is often accomplished by what we recognize as trade, or in its simplest sense, an exchange between nodes within the system. Now the process was being greatly sped up because the invitations were not limited to production or transportation. The speed with which these new products, ideas, and technologies could be disseminated to other countries and to other areas of the world had increased significantly. It no longer took generations for a meme to work its way from group to group in the slow process dictated by an agrarian system. Industrialization, with its rapid modes of transportation, moved these ideas throughout the system quickly. Capitalism was being transformed to a truly international system within decades. The technology that found its start in England was soon spreading throughout countries such as India, China, Africa, and the Americas.

Industrialization was a new period of chaos for the system. The production rates grew enormously over a short period of time. Other governments raced to catch up to England, and soon several countries were ramping-up their production. The next table shows this increase in five selected countries from the 1500 to 1900.

Rate of Industrial Growth

(Base Figures - 1905-13 = 100)

	UK	**France**	**Germany**	**Russia**	**Italy**
1781-90	3.8	10.9	-	-	-
1801-14	7.1	12.3	-	-	-
1825-34	18.8	21.5	-	-	-
1845-54	27.5	33.7	11.7	-	-
1865-74	49.2	49.8	24.2	13.5	42.9
1885-94	70.5	68.2	45.3	38.7	54.6
1905-13	100.0	100.0	100.0	100.0	100.0
% of world industrial production in 1913	14.0	6.4	17.7	5.5	2.7

From the Modern History source book, 2005

As with the sudden input from the beginning of farming over 10,000 years earlier, industrialization was causing the system to become unstable. Unlike that earlier period, there were now governments in place in all of these countries which would exert control over production. The first arms race was underway as production of goods for profit was quickly matched by other countries. The convergence of the three factors of land reform, technology, and abundant coal was driving Capitalism from its agrarian roots to become a profit-driven system. Markets had to be found to absorb the goods produced and maximize profits. Transportation was no longer the limiting factor. Soon, trains and steam ships would remedy that problem as Europe began building a new mechanized transport system to take their product to countries around the globe. The next table illustrates this rapid growth in rail systems.

Spread of Railroads in Ten Countries

(Length of line open [in kilometers [1km = 5/8 mile])

	1840	1860	1880	1900
Austria-Hungary	144	4,543	18,507	36,330
Belgium	334	1,730	4,112	4,591
France	496	9,167	23,089	38,109
Germany	469	11,089	33,838	51,678
Great Britain	2,390	14,603	25,060	30,079
Italy	20	2,404	9,290	16,429
Netherlands	17	335	1,846	2,776
Russia	27	1,626	22,865	53,234
Spain	-	1,917	7,490	13,214
Sweden	-	527	5,876	11,303

Reprinted from the Modern History Source Book, 2005

Surplus was now being generated for the specific purpose of moving it into new markets for profit. The quantities of surplus would move in the new transportation systems across oceans and land masses to find these new markets.

England, with its earlier start in mechanization over most of the countries of Europe, moved quickly to exploit this advantage by exporting to other countries as rapidly as possible. As a colonial power of the time, England utilized its colonies in the spreading of surplus. This would effectively lead it to tighten control over its colonial systems and to establish guidelines for regulation of trade along mercantilist lines. The colonies represented potential new export markets into which England could channel much of the massive output of goods being produced. At the same time, England began to institute the Staple Act, which required that any shipments of merchandise to the English colonies would have to be shipped through English ports. This made English goods cheaper for their colonies than other European goods. As industrialization continued, England was gradually creating a business class devoted to mercantilism and capitalist values. This was not the agrarian Capitalism that had evolved as a natural system along with human culture; this was a new Capitalism focused on and devoted to the creation of profit and the exploitation of markets. As the amount of surplus being produced by England continued to increase, the natural system of Capitalism suddenly found that one node of the system, England, was quickly becoming a major source of surplus for the entire system.

As we saw earlier with the study of chaos, a natural response would occur and the system tried to distribute this surplus to the other countries of Europe and the rest of the world. This was also not just the transfer of goods, but a transfer of culture and technology as we saw in our discussion of memes. Soon this system would began to form more complex connections as the cultural idea of industrialization was transmitted and found to be favorable by a majority of the nations. There would then follow synchronous activity, as dozens of countries moved rapidly toward industrialization and began producing large quantities of surplus in search of new markets. Market-driven Capitalism was now fully under way. The natural system had been driven to expansion globally. However, it was not without some significant drawbacks.

The rapid movement to redefined land ownership resulted in the displacement of large numbers of people. By the time we reached the 1700s in England, the poverty rate was above 50%. In agrarian Capitalism, there was stratification occurring as some groups would succeed and others would fail. In profit-driven Capitalism, the stratification was intensified as manufacturers worked to streamline the processes to maximize profit. This principal was fostered by the writings of Adam Smith in his *The Wealth of Nations,* where he proposed the only legitimate goal of national government and human activity was the steady increase in the overall wealth of the nation. Smith also pointed out, that while Capitalism, or the free market, often appeared chaotic and unrestrained, it was actually guided to produce the right amount by a so-called invisible hand. His work formed the basis of classical economic theory and also served as a valuable tool in the evolution of modern economics. Smith's guiding hand would be instrumental in directing governments in their attempts to control Capitalism. Just as Smith had envisioned, industrialization moved Capitalism beyond the individual, who had become insignificant. Government impacts on the system were intended to focus it on national output rather than the output of any single individual or group. The resulting intense stratification created distinct classes within human society. No longer was there the simple grouping of haves and have-nots, but distinctive social groups consisting of an aristocratic class, middle-class, and the poor. These are the social classes which come to be identified with Capitalism as we moved into the modern era. However, the social classes are a creation of governments and their drive toward control. Capitalism as a natural system does not seek to have, nor does it have the desire of a human being. It functioned in the period of industrialization much the same as it did with its evolution during the beginning of farming: as a system of moving surplus in exchange for benefit.

Competition by countries resulted in confrontation over new markets. For the front-running country, England, it brought direct confrontation with its colonies over the methods employed to distribute its surplus. By the late 1700s, the English government had imposed a series of taxes and restrictions on trade with in the colonies. The competition was a direct effort to restrict access to the system by colonies and restrict the manufacture of goods only to England. As long as England could maintain a virtual monopoly on trade with the colonies, it could keep prices high, but if the colonies were allowed to develop production means of their own, the cheaper sources of material available to them would reduce the price of goods. This is a problem we see in today's world with expansion into new developing countries. Very much in that same vein, the developed country will impose restrictions and tariffs in an attempt to control market access. The result is often the same: resentment, hostility, and eventually, rebellion.

The restrictions between England and her colonies took on an arcane and sometimes bizarre nature, as the English government imposed different acts in an effort to appease different members of the English constituency. One of these measures was the Hat Act, which prohibited the manufacture or construction of the hats within the colonies. The act specifically restricted uses of Blacks in the construction of hats. As a cheap labor source available to the colonies, but not to England, Blacks were a force that would help to lower construction costs for hats, ultimately lowering the price. That is the same parallel that we see today in many developing countries where cheap labor, cheap material, and means of production drive down prices for finished goods. The efforts of the English government to prevent this in the 1700s ended in very similar results to efforts by developed countries to restrict access to markets in today's world: there was rebellion and ultimately independence for the colonies. As these new governments came into being, they acted to protect their fledgling manufacturing efforts by raising similar taxes against each import into the colonies. It was not long before other countries began to raise similar tariffs against products produced outside of their countries. These tariffs were created primarily by governments to control the flow of capital. By restricting access of domestic markets to foreign countries, they hoped to control and maintain the flow of wealth in their own countries. The tariffs and other restrictive measures stopped the flow of surplus between individual countries by stopping the flow of products. The newly evolved global Capitalism was grinding to a halt as individual countries put up punitive tariffs to protect their industries and their national wealth from outside production sources. The system limped along through the latter part of the 1800s, but by the early portion of the 1900s, it almost completely wound down in the first global recession.

Part II
THE RIPPLE BECOMES A WAVE

Capitalism in the Era of International Trade

The behavior of the system at this time can be seen in an experiment conducted by Arthur Winfree in his description of biological oscillators. He conducted a very innovative thought experiment in which, instead of oscillators, he looked at the systems as if they consisted of people in a running club moving around a circular track. In reality, a circular track is exactly what Capitalism represents in the move to create surplus for profit, and returning again to generate more surplus. If one thinks of the nations of the world in the early 17th and 18th century as runners on the circular track, England would be an extremely tall runner, outdistancing the rest of the pack because it was the first to move into industrialization. The synchronous behavior which existed prior to this time would then begin to break up. As mentioned earlier, this type of natural system has a sensitivity based upon the relative inputs by each country operating as part of the system. When England made a leap forward, it moved away from the pack. However, Capitalism functioned as a transmitter of cultural (and in this case technical) information as exchanges of product began to occur between England and the other countries. In a very short period of time, other countries would begin to adjust their output. The system overcame the sensitivity and moved again toward synchronous behavior. The other runners caught up to England and the track now looks as if all the runners are again the same size. The transmission of this information occurs through memes as a vehicle of transmitting cultural and technical information throughout the natural system. The transmission of this information worked to keep the system in synchronous behavior and functioning smoothly.

The problem occurred when a competing system, governance, began to place obstacles in the way of this natural distribution of technology, product, and culture. The tariffs imposed acted to separate the individual countries so that synchronous activity was not possible. Each country was left to move around the track without relationship or connection to other countries. This did not only disrupt the flow of product but also began to disrupt the flow of technical information and cultural information between the various countries. This disruption was felt by every person in the system. For many generations, this period of time, the Depression, left an indelible mark upon their psyche. People from Europe and America had their behavior modified significantly because of the impact of this one event. So extensive was the global shutdown of the system, that no one country or group of countries could hope to correct the situation. To restart the system would require a global event, in this case, it was World War II. The global conflict began in the late 1930s and as hostilities escalated, countries began to crank up their international trade in response to this dispute. This global effort restored the system and again allowed output from individual nations to move freely around the globe. By this time, governments had begun to realize how important international trade was to global stability. When the conflict of World War II was finally resolved, the governments came together to address the problem of international trade.

Construction of the ideal

In 1947 in Breton Woods, New Hampshire, nations of the world came together to hold their first annual meeting to set up an economic blueprint for postwar recovery. Governments had come to recognize that international trade was too important to be left in the hands of individual nations. Representatives of United States, Great Britain, Russia, and 41 other nations created an accord which established the International Monetary Fund, the World Bank, and later in 1947, established the General Agreement on Tariffs and Trade, known as GATT. Each of these organizations is important, but of singular importance is the recognition of GATT as an agreement between nations of the world concerning international trade. At the time of its construction, the GATT agreement was to be an interim agreement and the GATT organization an interim one until a more permanent structure could be found. The nations agreed to establish an organization known as the International Trade Organization, or ITO. It was to be the organization to ensure there would be fairness in world trade and to resolve trade disputes between member countries and to provide protection and coverage for emerging countries in services and intellectual property. For the first time, governments were recognizing the existence of a natural system that required access to all markets to function properly. However, as with all things, there was some dissent. The United States, which has emerged from World War II as the dominant force, both militarily and economically, in the world, refused to sign in the regional agreement because of concerns about national security. Without the participation of this powerful production node, the International Trade Organization was doomed to failure, dying quietly within a few years of its creation. In its place was left the interim organization known as GATT. This organization, located in Berne, Switzerland, was opened to all countries, although it tended to be a Western-dominated organization. Many of the developing countries such as China and India were not members of the club. GATT represented government's awareness that protection of the natural system superseded national boundaries. As the war had ended and gross domestic product for the world had increased significantly, the need for a permanent organization and structure to ensure the smooth flow of product and technological information passed along by the natural system of Capitalism had to occur. As shown in this next table, Global Gross Domestic Product (GDP) was again racing ahead.

World GDP 1500-1992

Date	*World GDP(a)*
1500	100
1820	290
1870	470
1900	823
1913	1,136
1929	1,540
1950	2,238
1973	6,693
1992	11,664

Source: Maddison 1995:19, 227.

From *Something New Under the Sun* by J.R. McNeil, Paul Kennedy: A Environmental History of the Twentieth century World by Norton 2001

GATT became the controlling mechanism to ensure that trade disputes did not interrupt international trade. It would continue to function in this capacity until 1994.

During the Uruguay round of multilateral trade negotiations a new organization was created, the World Trade Organization (WTO), to take over much of the responsibility for handling disputes. The WTO was to be the world form for handling trade disputes and disagreements which would disrupt flow within the global marketplace. The first six paragraphs of the organizing principles for the WTO are reprinted here.

> *Recognizing that their relations in the field of trade and economic endeavor should be conducted with a view to raising standards of living, ensuring full employment and a large and steadily growing volume of real income and effective demand, and expanding the production and trade in goods and services, while allowing for the optimal use of the world's resources in accordance with the objective of sustainable development, seeking both to protect and preserve the environment and enhance the means for dong so in a manner consistent with their respective needs and concerns at different levels of economic development,*
>
> *Recognizing further that there is need for positive efforts designed to ensure that developing countries, and especially the least developed among them, secure a share in the growth in international trade commensurate with the needs of their economic development,*

Being desirous of contributing to these objectives by entering into reciprocal and mutually advantageous arrangements directed to the substantial reduction of tariffs and other barriers to trade and to the elimination of discriminatory treatment in international trade relations,

Resolved, therefore, to develop an integrated, more viable and durable multilateral trading system encompassing the General Agreement on Tariffs and Trade, the results of past trade liberalization efforts, and all of the results of the Uruguay Round of multilateral trade negotiation, Determined to preserve the basic principles and to further the objectives underlying this multilateral trading system,

Agree as follows:

Article I

Establishment of the Organization The World Trade Organization (hereinafter referred to as "the WTO") is hereby established.

This new organization was highly controversial, but countries had begun to recognize that nations were no longer the important factor in global trade. As pointed out by Winfree in his analysis of biological oscillators, as global input returned to normal and the system of Capitalism began to function again, no nation was indispensable. The important factor was to maintain the operation of the natural system and the global marketplace. Establishment of the World Trade Organization was supposed to achieve this end. It was the form where governments would go to resolve trade disputes and discourage trade wars. The WTO, which was also headquartered in Geneva, was headed by a ministerial conference, which has a one-country-one-vote body. This gave small and developing countries the same voice, in theory, as the larger more developed countries. There were specific dispute resolution procedures in place for handling trade disputes and an appellate review process to allow appeal from unfavorable decisions. Although the WTO had no power to bind the countries, the countries themselves recognized the importance of having such an organization in place.

Two other organizations, the World Bank and International Monetary Fund (IMF), came into existence at the same time and were to prove critical in maintaining the stability of the global system. The World Bank and IMF would be the primary funding resources to make sure that developing countries would have access to the moneys they needed to modernize and move into the new century. Along with these organizations came a final umbrella organization known as the United Nations. It was to be the grand meetinghouse of countries where they could come to discuss problems and work out disputes instead of going to war with each other. These organizations were the ideal in terms of what was supposed to happen to protect the global marketplace.

The Reality

Disputes created before the start of World War II began to blossom into a new type of confrontation after the war, a Cold War. The forces of East and West had polarized themselves into two opposing camps of ideology, communism, and democracy. These camps would set the agenda for global behavior until the 1990s. In reality, this was a confrontation between the two different systems of economics. The Communist countries and those in their sphere of influence were proponents of Karl Marx's theory of managed economies. On the other side were the forces of democracy with their purported adherence to free trade and open systems. In between these two warring factions was the natural system of Capitalism, the system which had worked with human culture for over 10,000 years.

Despite the restrictions on trade imposed by the conflict between these two warring factions, Capitalism found a way to extend itself, even into the countries controlled by Communists. The transmission of cultural ideas and technology could not now be limited by the advent of government systems to restrict such flow. However, it could be severely curtailed. In the Communist Bloc countries controlled by the Soviet Union, Capitalism was an underground system functioning along side the government's attempt to provide a managed and socialist system. Pockets of entrepreneurial enterprise would spring up in the most unusual places. Criminal activity and the existence of criminal cartels kept the natural system of Capitalism alive in these regions. Underground black markets moved excess product from the West into the environs of the Soviet Union where it was readily consumed. Even members of the Communist Party used these systems to procure luxury items and other material not available in a communist system. Capitalism was finding a way to accommodate itself to the new political realities. This unofficial black market would also foster the spread of cultural ideas and new technologies as they became available.

And in the Western world, Capitalism was to be a standard practice of the democratic countries. In schools and universities throughout the United States and Europe, economists would praise Capitalism as a direct offshoot of democracy. While the Soviet Union was seen as gray and repressive, the Western societies were full of color and vigor. Capitalism found a more willing following in the Western societies than it did in the Soviet Union. However, neither of these two governments were prepared to deal with the emergence of developing nations.

As we saw when industrialization began and England began to move massive quantities of products into its colonies, there was a natural creation of competition. Colonists began to duplicate the English model, which had been successful, and establish their own manufacturing around cheaper material and cheaper sources of labor. This immediately created a conflict as the developed country of England wanted to keep prices high and the colonies wanted to reduce those prices with cheaper manufacturing. The same age-old conflict began to occur between Western countries, the Soviet Union, and developing countries. In Africa, South America, India, and China, populations were being excluded from active participation in Capitalism. The system was being artificially manipulated to keep these countries and their huge impact on the resultant price of goods from moving fully into the system. As we can see in the next table, world population had grown dramatically and with it, the driving force for Capitalism and the products it could make available.

World Population Growth 1804-1992

1 billion 1804

2 billion 1927 (123 years later)

3 billion 1960 (33 years later)

4 billion 1974 (14 years later)

5 billion in 1987 (13 years later)

Source Data Book 1999

This pressure to spread information and equalize the system by spreading Capitalism throughout the developing countries brought it into conflict not only with the Soviet Union, but also with the Western democracies. To allow uncontrolled and unfettered access to the technologies that would bring these masses of people into the marketplace would do irreparable harm to the Democratic economies, or so it was believed. As always, there was the increasing need for security. As the '40s moved into the '50s, the different ideologies met on the battlefield of Korea. As we move into the decade of the '60s,'70s, and '80s, they confronted each other globally. These military conflicts were only small part of the struggle going on behind the scenes between both of these government types, and Capitalism.

In China, there was growing tension with the Soviet Union, its primary ally. With a growing population, China desperately needed technology. The Soviet Union would often provide technical assistance, but only of a limited nature. Sharing a large continuous border with China made military concerns more important than the transmission of cultural, technical, and social information.

India, the world's largest democracy and a relatively new state on the world scene, gravitated more toward the Soviet camp than Western democracies. India had a longstanding history with one of the principles of democracy, Britain, who had controlled India for over 50 years. This domination by a Western power had left many in the Indian government untrusting of Western governments. With a population rivaling that of China, India, too, had a great need to obtain technology to move it into the age of industrialization and the modern world.

Yet, what was provided by the developed nations was often limited by the continuing need of national security. The Soviet Union, embroiled in a cold war with the West, had a primary responsibility to protect its own population. It did not allow the free flow of information as Capitalism would dictate; the aide rendered was often second- and third-line material rather than top-of-the-line Soviet technology. Likewise, as the Soviet Union began to spread its influence all round the world into countries such as in Africa, it was more willing to provide small arms and dated weapons systems rather than technology that would move economies into the future.

Although loudly exclaiming the virtues of free trade, the Western democracies where doing little more than the Soviet Union. During the ’50s, ’60s, and ’70s, the primary Western democracy, the United States, was locked in a series of conflicts with the Soviet Union. Its focus was on building nuclear weapons and restricting trade to its arch rival that might shift the military advantage. During this time, the Western governments made overtures to India, Africa, and to a limited degree, China. These efforts were largely in the form of minimal economic aid and very limited technology transfers.

The institutions which had been so carefully crafted after World War II to protect and ensure free movement of goods and services across international boundaries had been hopelessly corrupted by the realities of the modern world. The World Trade Organization, founded in ’90s with a specific purpose of creating an international forum to resolve trade disputes, was increasingly insensitive to the fears held by many members regarding issues of the loss of national sovereignty. The sensitivities were only exacerbated when the Director General for the World Trade Organization make statements indicating the intent of the organization to create a single global economy. The organization had an additional weakness when it came to the disparate size of the countries belonging to the organization; there was no way to reconcile the differences in input, both economic and physical. Countries such as the United States were often inflamed by the one-country-one-vote rule. U.S. representatives argued for the creation of a second body similar to the U.S. House of Representatives where size mattered. Also, the World Trade Organization also had no enforcement capability. Its decisions were non-binding, depending largely upon the willingness of participating countries to adhere to decisions rendered by the Organization. Regional agreements have further weakened the ability of the World Trade Organization to function. The establishment of the North American Free Trade Agreement and the European Union are regional concerns that largely ignored the existence of the World Trade Organization. However, it is not the only organization with severe shortcomings in being able to ensure that international trade would proceed unhindered.

The United Nations, the seminal organization for promoting international discourse in the resolution of disputes, has likewise found itself rendered largely impotent by modern considerations. The United Nations General Assembly operates on the same principle as the World Trade Organization, where every country gets an equal voice. Again, this one-country-one-vote policy has always proved an irritant and a stumbling block to full and unfettered participation by developed countries, such as the United States, Britain, France, and Russia. Because of this, resolutions from the General Assembly are often at odds with global considerations of the major powers. In an effort to prevent an outbreak of democracy within the United Nations, the Security Council was the final brake on actions by the General Assembly. The Security Council had five positions reserved for the developing countries, with one seat rotating between the other nations over a fixed period of time. In this manner, the developed countries could override any action by the United Nations that was deemed inappropriate. There was also the additional issue of funding, with most of it coming from the developed countries. He who controls the purse strings has the power of the golden rule: the man with the gold makes the rule.

The organizations set up to provide interim and long-term funding to developing countries were likewise converted into instruments of control to be used by the developed countries to contain and regulate growth in the developing countries. The International Monetary Fund, which was created at the same time as the World Bank and GATT, was intended to be a financing mechanism to consider macro economic performance and financial sector policies in developing countries. The IMF is the short-term lending arm, and the World Bank provides long-term financing to developing countries. These organizations are largely funded by developed countries, as illustrated in the next table, and the agenda put forward is designed to preserve the status between developed countries and developing countries.

Ten Largest Contributors

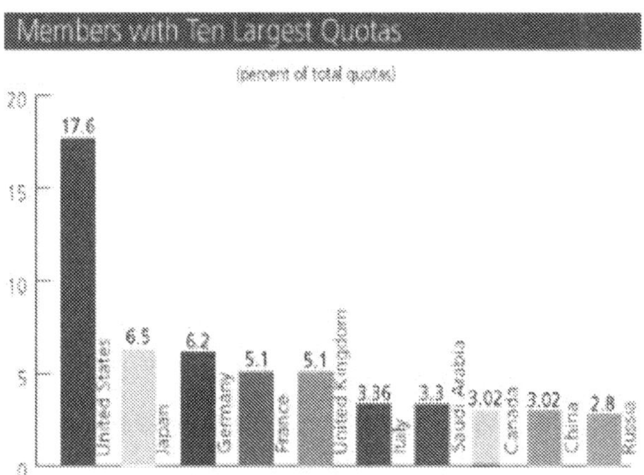

http://www.imf.org/external/pubs/ft/exrp/what.htm#origins

In many cases, lending from these institutions is predicated on requiring developing countries to privatize resources including water supplies, public utilities, banking, and natural resources such as petroleum in order to receive loans. As of 2005, the result has been that in countries such as Bolivia, after 25 years of loans, personal income in the country has actually fallen. As a result, we begin to see countries in the developing world moving away from the West and pursuing individual agendas to protect their resources and their economies from what they believe to be further exploitation by the developed countries.

For an example of this exploitation, we have only to look to the ongoing negotiations with in the United Nations in what is called "the Doha round." The negotiations began to hammer out a balance between developed countries' trade restrictions on manufactured goods and farm products from developing countries and the need of these developing countries to have access to markets of developed countries. The negotiations have been underway for many years without success. At one point, the principle stumbling block was the U.S. provision to provide agricultural subsidies to its farmers in order to protect the farm industry of the United States. In the last round of negotiations taking place in 2005 in Hong Kong, the United States came forward with recommendations which were rejected by developing countries. The proposal offered a vague, staggered phase-out of subsidies over two distinct time periods far in the future. There was no specific timetable for the termination of agricultural subsidies by the United States or the European Union. By keeping the farm produce of these poor countries out of the international marketplace, they depress the economies of those nations and reduced their ability to provide for their people. The United States and European Union have kept the subsidies in place to protect the agricultural business sector of their countries. At the same time, a group of developing countries attempted to negotiate a rewrite of the rules dealing with service industries which handle express package delivery and insurance in the developing countries. Most of this business is operated and controlled by companies based in Europe and North America. The changes were designed to restrict some access by the developed countries to these types of industries and to offer some degree of protection for fledgling industries in the developing countries, just as it was offered in the United States and Europe to agribusiness. The proposal was soundly rejected by the developing countries.

There has also been ongoing dispute between the Western nations and the developing world about control of international systems such as the Internet. This global communication network, which handles huge quantities of information on a daily basis, has become an international asset. Yet, control of the underlying structure for the Internet rest solely in the hands of a nonprofit corporation controlled by the United States government. In 2005, the developing nations, this time joined by the European Union, were engaged in a hotly contested debate over whether the one country should control the system or whether there should be an international consortium to handle rulemaking and structure for the Internet. Despite increasing international pressure, the United States continues to control the infrastructure for the Internet. It is instances like this that keep the developing countries outside of the international marketplace in many significant aspects.

These factors operate in opposition to the natural system that we have been discussing. Capitalism, as with most complex systems, works to redistribute pressure, or surplus, and to create uniformity between nodes present within the system. It is one reason for Capitalism's success in spreading throughout human populations. It acts as a facilitator for the spread of culture and technological information, as well as finished goods and services between differing groups. As the system has evolved into a global network, it has tended to resist the limitations of governments to restrict access by some nodes as opposed to others. Capitalism wants to disseminate ideas between all groups, something that governments will not allow.

Capitalism is a very resourceful system and will seek to maintain its own survival as a functioning system. When the two large government blocks put up barriers to its continuous global operation, the system found other means of fulfilling its primary goal of the transmission of surplus in exchange for benefit/profit. It found a lucrative and well entrenched underground network of black markets and criminal cartels. What the two major political powers would not provide openly, the developing countries sought through unofficial means. As a result, China and India both acquired nuclear weapons and technology to produce and develop new series of weapons.

Africa became a hotbed of underground activity in diamonds and drugs. Capitalism was working its way around the barricade set up by government. In the 60s, Capitalism was to find a new and vital ally in its struggle for survival against governments: technology.

The Age of Electronics

As the East and West stalked each other in political conflict and the developing countries struggled to obtain information and material for their economies as best they could, a small group of scientists in New Jersey were about to make a discovery that would fundamentally change the world and Capitalism. John Bardeen, William Shockley, and Walter Brattain were scientists at the Bell Telephone Laboratories in Murray Hill, New Jersey. They had been working for a long period of time on a method of replacing cumbersome and fragile vacuum tubes in electronic systems. Vacuum tubes consumed a great deal of power and were very difficult to ship. Even when the glass enclosure was replaced by metal, they were still bulky and difficult to store. This team had been working for a period of time in this effort and was about to give up when they decided to try a last-ditch attempt using a purer substance as a contact point. This last effort led them to the use of semiconductor materials. This process would be known as the transistor. For these three men, it would earn them the Nobel Prize in Physics; for the world, it would forever change communication. From 1956 on, the use of transistors opened up the new world of electronics manufacture and design, which would eventually lead to the development of cheap computers. These cheap computers would make it possible for individuals to engage in activities which were heretofore prohibited because of the time and effort it would take. Calculations of a complex nature were first done with banks of large-scale computers, which would ever decrease in size as we move from the transistor into integrated circuits. Eventually, this innovation would lead to the construction of a network of communication which is today known as the Internet.

The Internet makes it possible for large amounts of information to be communicated on a worldwide basis through its network. As the Internet developed, it became a method for the rapid transmission of Capitalism. Capitalism is more than the transmission of goods; it is also the transmission of ideas, themes, and concepts. The Internet made it possible to propagate these ideas, or memes, to many different segments of society and cultures all around the world. As the Internet grew in importance, it became more difficult for any government or group of governments to restrict the flow of information and Capitalism. By the time we reached the '90s, Capitalism, which had been forced underground in many portions of communist countries, had blossomed into established and recognized models for conducting commerce. The Internet was to a large degree responsible for this. As industrialization had made the individual irrelevant, so the age of the Internet rendered national borders irrelevant.

The Internet is a system known as a small world network. The universe is full of these types of networks in biology, mathematics, social structures, and man-made systems such as the Internet. Like most of the systems, there are three critical components, or tendencies, which can best describe the system. In the case of small world networks, they are: short chains, high clustering, and scale-free link distributions. Scale-free simply means that the system is not dominated by any single representative scale. Steven Strogatz provided an excellent example of this in his book *Sync*. If you look at the average height of human beings around the world, it will fall around five feet. Therefore, human heights have a characteristic scale of five feet. This is a perfect example of a scale free system. The scale-free principle was first pointed out by Laszlo Barbasi and his students Reka Albert and Hawoong Jeong in their probing of the World Wide Web. He pointed out that such systems exhibit behavior which can be categorized as bearing a stamp of natural selection. The Internet was the perfect vehicle for expansion of Capitalism; it was the blending of two kindred spirits. Just as in Capitalism, small networks are robust with respect to random failures, but fragile when subjected to selective targeting. In the world at large, the systems can survive any number of natural occurrences and continue functioning. However, the fragility of the systems becomes apparent when they are selectively attacked a specific points intentionally. This is not only the sensitivity of the Internet, but also of Capitalism. These results were compiled by Barbasi and his team in looking at two different databases. The first data base look at connectivity data where two proteins were regarded as linked if one is known to bind to the other, then they correlated the connectivity data with the results of the systematic mutation experiments in which biologists had previously deleted certain proteins to see if their removal would be lethal to the cell. Cells are buffered against the loss of most of their individual proteins, just as small networks are buffered against the lost of individual nodes. This is similar to the way Capitalism works: no person or country is indispensable.

In a flurry of activities, countries scrambled to try to get control of this new medium and to put in place consensus agreements for handling the rapidly spreading system. By the time we reached the new millennium, this system had spread Capitalism without respect to governments, communist or democracy, to almost every place on earth. The rapid spread of communications made it possible for the exchange of information, technologies, and culture, often in disregard to the wishes of various governments. However, this new transition into a global network, or "globalization" as it is called, did not relieve some of the age-old problems which had been created during World War II. Capitalism ignores persons and nations and works to disseminate information, technologies, and culture throughout the system. As a system, the sensitivity factor which dominates is the need to be sure of that each node within the complex network is more or less uniform in terms of its input into the network. This ensures that no node is indispensable. Governments, on the other hand, have been racing to attempt to catch up and to control the system so as to restrict this flow of information. However, they have begun to recognize the importance of being sure the network is stable. This has created a significant amount of friction between global Capitalism and social priorities.

The Clash of Capitalism and Social Systems

In the Western countries, World War II brought another change. Unions, which had been struggling to gain footholds in the United States, found the advent of global conflict very advantageous. The need for workers put them in an excellent position to recruit members and to be able to promise economic fulfillment for their members. From the latter portion of the 19th century until the 20th century, unions had become a safe haven for many minorities within the United States. They offered the promise of equal employment and equal opportunity. It was in this context that unions made a fateful decision during World War II: they adopted the idea of social reform. The first of these reforms was pensions.

Before this time, pensions had been offered to specific groups of people, such as serving officers in military organizations such as the British Navy and Union soldiers having served in the Civil War. In both cases, the pensions were small and poorly administered. The second group consisted of business executives working for the newly evolving international conglomerates. Pensions were a valuable tool for this group. Pensions allowed them to offer attractive packages to individuals without actually having to pay the money up front. Since pensions could be deferred until some later date, such as separation or retirement, they often were only listed in secret agreements in the corporation. American Express offered the first pension back in 1875. Soon after that, other corporations began to offer comparable tie pensions for their executives, and over the next 20 years, states and cities added pensions to police officers and firefighters. In the 20th century, pensions became a tool of social policy when unions began to adopt the concept in their negotiating strategy with corporations. During World War II, this proved to be beneficial to unions since there were wage caps in place. In order to attract skilled workers, offering benefits was desirable for both management and the unions. Corporations only had to negotiate with one group of people to keep the work force stable. This allowed the corporations to direct most of their efforts toward war production rather than negotiating contracts. The unions recognized this as a way of being able to offer their members the promise of economic security: they would be entitled to a pension which would make their life in old age secure. The corporations loved it because it was the promise of future payments that would be dealt with far down the road, if at all. Once this social engineering began, unions then moved into other areas in order to keep the stream of promises flowing and the ranks of their membership growing.

It was not long after the war ended that unions began to seek other considerations: a limit on the number of hours workers would be required to work in a given day, the work week shortened to five days, and medical and educational benefits became part of the negotiating package. For minorities, unions also offered a source of funding to create a balance in the political system itself. Many activities in the early stages of Civil Rights were supported financially and physically by unions. In no small part, Civil Rights owes its success to unions.

This process of offering benefit packages was an attractive lure used to increase the numbers of workers with union membership. In the 1950s and ‘60s, union membership reached an all-time high in United States with 45% of the private work force belonging to unions. The promise of these social programs of pensions, medical payments, and social reform attracted many members to union ranks. However, the problem with pensions is one of concept. The social programs put into place ignored economic realities. It was a promise today for payments 40 to 50 years down the road when economic conditions could not be forecasted. Also, there were no safeguards in place to force corporations to fully fund pension plans and keep them secure. However, it was economic insecurity which would prove the downfall of this social engineering concept.

By the time we reach the ’80s and ’90s, Capitalism and global production hit new records. Markets within the Western world were becoming saturated and there was a need for Western companies to begin seeking new markets in the developing countries in order to keep their profit margins growing. This would require an exchange of not only product but of technology and money. This change would prompt developing countries to begin more actively seeking to emulate, or copy, the Capitalist system which had brought such prosperity to the West. As we saw at the beginning of the Industrial Revolution, production facilities would develop in the developing countries, which often had cheaper materials and cheaper pools of labor. In order to make use of these commodities, outsourcing, or sending work to Third World countries where it could be done more cheaply, became an attractive tool. Wal-Mart, one of the economic giants of the 20th was a pioneer in this respect. However, the net result of this activity was to begin to draw down wages in the Western world as more and more work was moved to developing countries with cheaper labor and materials. This placed an undue strain on many Western corporations as global competition began to heat up, and developing countries such as China, India, and countries in South America and Africa began to compete for the international market. Added to this was a downturn in markets within the United States during the late 1990s. As Western companies scrambled to adjust to this new economic reality, it became clear that pensions were no longer viable. Many companies in the West phased out their pension plans for new workers, eliminating pension plans for workers that were not tested, and reduced pension plans and medical benefits for vested workers. Many companies, such as General Motors, Ford Motor, Hewlett-Packard, and a growing list of other companies, were following suit. In response to this economic reality, there were outcries from many sectors for social balance on the part of corporations, but there was little the corporations could actually do. Economic realities and underfunding of pension plans for long periods of time made it virtually impossible for the corporations or the governments to maintain plans at their current levels. The West was feeling the effects of this phase of expansion in much the same way England had during industrialization.

Capitalism was working hard to bring the global system into alignment by equalizing prices and production. Governments, however, saw this differently as their citizens brought pressure to correct the situation. Yet, the pressure of global Capitalism was unstoppable. During the 21st century, programs were going into place in recognition of the globalization of world markets. Europe was forming itself into the European Union to be more effective in reducing barriers within Europe and in competing with other power centers globally. The United States was likewise trying to craft out a North American version of this process with programs such as the North American Free Trade Act (NAFTA) and the Central American Free Trade Act (CAFTA). The provisions of these acts did not rest easily with populations within the Western world who found themselves displaced by global competition.

Despite the fact that in much of the rest of the world the social programs, which are so prevalent and engrained in the West, are virtually unknown. Pensions are few and far between in China, India, Africa, or South America. Despite the fact that the Western democracies represented less than one sixth of the world population, they now effectively controlled 60 to 70% of the economic and technological capacity of the world. This clash between social systems and Capitalism simply added fuel to the fire, creating more discord between governments, social systems, and Capitalism.

Capitalism had always created stratification in populations. In its early stages, agrarian Capitalism had created haves and have-nots in the Fertile Crescent. Industrialization magnified this process and created three distinct social classes within much of Western culture. Although these classes were largely crafted by governments, they have become associated with Capitalism. As technology fueled the latest rapid modification of Capitalism in the age of information technology, we see a further stratification occurring. The World was quickly being split into two very different economic models. The developed countries had moved past heavy manufacturing into what they called the service sector economy. In these countries, technology was in full bloom and they were the sponsors and developers of ideas, theories, and technologies. Heavy manufacturing, the dirty business of creating things, was shifted to the developing countries of China, India, and many countries of Africa and South America. Despite the inconsistency in the two models, the developing countries were beginning to make great strides in moving themselves through industrialization and into the global marketplace. The unofficial system of Capitalism, the black market, had served the developing countries well in helping them obtain the transfers of technology that were needed to move their economies forward. In a matter of a few short years, they were moving from sweat shops into the era of modern production facilities. Despite the best effort of Western technicians to craft this system as two separate economic models, the developing countries would not cooperate. Capitalism and the natural flow of information it engenders was their staunchest ally in moving them from simply being permanent places of poverty and manufacturing to supply Western civilizations into true global competitors in the international markets. However, the conflict between the two groups continues to intensify.

The question we face as we move into the 21st century is how will Capitalism, this natural system, continue to effect human behavior? Once we have reached the point where developing countries can compete effectively with Western economies, will the system simply be allowed to settled down into a period of new synchronicity and stability, or will interference by governments create new instabilities? What will the system look like in the future?

Part III:

The System at Maturity

An Old Friend or a New Enemy

Capitalism has changed from the simple agrarian system of surplus exchange created with the advent of farming to the market-driven system it evolved into as a result of industrialization to its present form as the primary conveyor-system for the transmission of technologies and capital. This final stage, happening as result of Capitalism finding, once again, favorable technologies in the form of the Internet. The global communication systems of the Internet have proved an invaluable tool in aiding in the spread of Capitalism on a global basis. The system has survived for many thousands of years because of the simplicity of its construction, its robust nature as a natural system, and the ease with which it can be transmitted and replicated. As we saw in the beginning with the agrarian start of Capitalism, surplus is a key identifying factor for this type of system. The need to exchange that surplus in some fashion to obtain benefit completes the picture for the system. As it has worked with human culture, it has undergone significant change. In its final stages, Capitalism has come to face its most daunting ally: world governments. The nature of the system is such that it wants to spread, or disseminate, pressure, information, technologies, products, or cultural attitudes throughout the network it has created. In that regard, Capitalism is a more altruistic system than we might at first expect. The pressure created by its need to find new markets creates the perfect vehicle for the distribution of culture and technologies. As populations have increased, so has the drive generated within the system to affect distribution among the individual nations with in the network.

This can most clearly be seen in the case of several countries that have risen rapidly from agricultural status to technological marketer within the time frame of a few decades. China is one of those countries. Today, it is the second largest economy in the world. Scarcely 20 years ago, China was considered little more than an over-populated, backward communist country. In the short period of time since then, it has been the recipient of the exchange created by Capitalism. Wal-Mart, a private capitalist company, was to be the vehicle for this exchange. In order to compete in a world where profit margins were growing thinner each year, Wal-Mart developed a scheme that would allow it to find and develop a huge untapped source of cheap labor. Not only were the workers of China a cheap labor force, but they were highly skilled and highly motivated. The government, although communist, was eager to find and develop new sources of technology for its people. A natural exchange was taking place. Wal-Mart would find its source of cheap and highly skilled labor and at the same time, it would affect a transfer with China of financial support, technology, and access to world markets. For both of these groups, it was a marriage made in heaven. Wal-Mart quickly began to establish an ongoing relationship with the Chinese government to create manufacturing facilities within China, the output of which would be sold in United States. These products of high-quality and low price were ideal for the emerging U.S. marketplace. This model works so well that dozens of U.S. and European companies rushed to imitate it. Soon there were dozens of countries beginning to form relationships with China in order to tap the huge resources of that labor force. These were not just retail stores but some of the greatest names in technology also found their way to China. In an effort to make use of the new financial and technological assets at its disposal, China became active in requiring these investors to transfer technologies and to create Chinese companies. By the time we reached 2005, China has successfully transformed itself into a global economic power based on technology. The skylines of Chinese cities were quickly beginning to rival that of metropolitan cities in the Western world. China had become capitalist. The system of exchange put into place between China and Western companies for the creation of surplus for profit had served to spur this country's growth.

Another example of explosive growth as a result of Capitalism is the nation of India. Again, Western companies began actively seeking to cultivate the developing markets within this country, which resulted in an exchange of moneys and technologies with India. India is the world's largest democracy, but because of its past relationship with Western governments, it has often been friendlier to communist countries than democracies. None of that mattered to

Capitalism; its only goal was to create surplus and to affect the exchange of materials and knowledge necessary to receive benefit. India is a rising economy and a growing source of technological manpower and expertise. India has stated its goal to become a supplier of highly skilled technicians, engineers, scientists, doctors, and business managers for the growing global business market. The Indian business community has recognized that people have become simple commodities in the capitalist system to be traded like any other commodity. India operates several of the largest schools in the world for the training of scientists and engineers, their graduation rate of trained professionals on a par with the United States and Europe. The system of Capitalism has affected an exchange between countries that produce quantities of human capital and the growing need within the global community for technical expertise. This is not the only country which is utilizing human capital as a prime commodity for the global marketplace.

Cuba, the small and impoverished communist country off the coast of the United States, has been using human capital as a primary medium of exchange for years. Cuba produces large numbers of highly skilled and trained doctors and nurses from its universities each year. In Cuba, these individuals earn salaries of approximately $25 a month. The Cuban government has often required graduates from medical schools to work from six months to a year in portions of South America providing services to the poor as a way to help pay for Cuban oil imports. Salaries for these professionals in South America average $350 a month. This is a substantial increase to the wages they can earn in Cuba. The government has recently begun to increase enrollment in its medical schools so that it will have a larger supply of doctors and nurses with which to trade.

This use of human beings as capital may seem somewhat unsettling to some, however, it is a natural outgrowth in the evolution of Capitalism in its current form. The system recognizes that people, and the ideas and intellect that they carry with them, are critical commodities. Where there is surplus of these commodities, the system works to move this surplus to where it can be exchanged for profit. This is the way that the natural system works. As we discussed earlier, Capitalism is what is known as a small world network, characterized by short chains, clumping, and being scale-free. This trilogy of fundamental characteristics is typical for these types of systems. It doesn't matter whether you're looking at systems of oscillators, the synchronous flashing of fireflies, the complexity of the human mind, the human genome, or the complexity of the Internet, they are all one in the same: small world networks of complexity and connectivity. As we began to move away the coverings from the systems, the underlying structure is the same. They are nodes assembled in a network of diverse connectivity. This reduces the system to its simplest and most basic form. All the systems tend to exhibit three fundamental characteristics of varying types that can be used to describe them. At the heart of each of these systems is connectivity, the need to create some type of exchange between the nodes of the system. The result of this exchange is a balance of the system. Capitalism does this as effectively and robustly as any other natural system. Connectivity is not without its price. Where there is connectivity, surplus, and profit, there'll also be economic shifts that will occur.

Capitalism has always created stratification. Whether it is in the valley of the Fertile Crescent, the industrialized cities of England, or the massive network of global communications we called the Internet, the effort to move surplus in exchange for profit will often mean that someone will lose as the system works to balance surplus throughout the network. When we talk about it in the abstract, this does not seem so bad. When you consider it in real terms, with each node being a country with millions of inhabitants been affected by this transfer and redistribution, it is different. The exchange of surplus throughout the system as required by Capitalism will affect Western nations more dramatically than the poor nations. The wealthy nations of Europe and the United States represent 60% of global wealth. Capitalism seeks to redistribute that wealth and technology to poorer nations. We see this occurring in the exchanges happening between China and the West and India and the West. These are the two greatest examples of the change taking place. As this occurs, there is a resultant decrease in wages and assets in the West, which corresponds to a resultant increase in wages and assets in countries such as China. In purely theoretical terms, the decrease in wages and increase in wages should meet at some point and eventually stop. However, this is little solace to the individual worker in United States or Europe who has lost a job to downsizing due to outsourcing. This, however, is the process of Capitalism. The interesting fact is that the process has been amplified by the resistance of governments to allow the system to work as it was intended. It is not just the Western cultures who are experiencing the trauma associated with the system's attempts to spread surplus, whether jobs or people, to where they are needed.

I remember recently observing job creation developments in China. There was one location shown on the news of a government-run hiring facility in a specific province. I followed activities there over a period of time. In the early portion of the 21st century, 2001 and 2002, there were long lines outside of the government office as employers could pick and choose from large groups of skilled workers waiting in line for the opportunity to work. By the time we reached 2004 and looked again at the same office, there were no lines outside, and only one or two workers inside talking to individuals of the various facilities. In every case, the individuals were not desperate for a job but were shopping to see who was paying the highest wages or offering a better benefits package. Even though China has a large population, it is not infinite. In a rather rapid fashion, China had begun to absorb all the available skilled workers. Many employers within the country are finding themselves in a position comparable to American companies as they struggle to find additional workers to satisfy their needs. The other factor is increasing competition from India for the lucrative contracts with Wal-Mart, IBM, and other Western companies. As the pool of skilled workers has begun to dry up in China, the system has shifted its focus to India where there may be greater surpluses of skilled laborers.

Governments in the West, in an effort to protect industries and to protect their assets in the same way that nations did during mercantilism, placed restrictions on trade in opposition to the forces of Capitalism. Capitalism is robust and can survive any number of natural events from wars, disease, and natural disasters, but it is very susceptible to a direct attack on individual nodes within the system. This system frailty resulted in the global collapse of the 1920s as restraints on trade imposed by governments brought Capitalism to a standstill. Although governments now understand that global trade must be allowed to proceed without restraint or interference, they often feel compelled to interfere because of political pressure, yet these efforts often do more to intensify the problem than to solve it. Placing restrictions on trade is often seen as an effort by the West to create a world in which there are rich nations perpetually and poor nations perpetually.

One of the questions I often asked students in my ethics classes in 2004 is about global fairness. The population of the Western world, including Europe and the United States, totals some 700 million people. The global population for the whole world represents 7 billion people. I asked my students if they think it is fair for a minority to oppress a majority. In every case, the general response to such a general question is "no." When I ask them if they would be willing to give up their standard of living to keep people in Africa, South America, India, or China from starving, they are quick to say "yes" until they have had a moment to reflect on the question, then the answer inevitably becomes "no." You can often see in their eyes the dawning of uncertainty as they become unsure about how much they're willing to give up to the rest of the world. If you were to ask those same questions in Mexico, China, or India, I am sure you would get very similar responses as those countries are now beginning to move successfully into the global marketplace. Capitalism doesn't require or demand, it simply goes about its business of redistributing surplus in order to reduce system pressure at any one node. If you are the recipient of that distribution, it is wonderful. But, as history will teach us all too soon, it may become your time to give up something rather than to receive something. It is at that point that we often have the difficulty accepting how the system works. Perhaps it is more a statement of the maturity of our species, or the lack thereof, than anything else.

What we cannot ignore is the reality that the world needs Capitalism. We have become so intertwined with the system that it is unthinkable for the world to continue without it. As Dawkins pointed out in his discussion on memes, there is a proponent of the survival of the fittest when we look at cultural systems. Capitalism has earned its place as a survivor. More importantly, the system is irreplaceable in today's economic scheme. The creation of market-driven systems are fundamental to the economic well-being of all societies. Countries that are poor look toward Capitalism as a way of reversing the poverty and entering the global marketplace successfully. There are numerous examples of that as pointed out earlier. However, there is a growing trend which looks away from Capitalism and toward other models for the creation of successful economies.

In South America, there's a growing trend away from globalization and market-driven economies. Venezuela is one such society. There, the government has begun an aggressive implementation of social reform to combat that nation's crippling poverty. Despite having large reserves of petroleum, Venezuela has been one of the many nations in South America that has yet to realize economic prosperity. It has chosen to align itself with countries such as Cuba and the philosophy of managed economic systems rather than Capitalism. A number of other countries in South America are beginning to follow suit, including Bolivia, one of the poorest nations in that region.

Although the governments of these nations look away from globalization, the underlying system of Capitalism still exists and flourishes within these countries. What we have here is a debate about agrarian Capitalism verses the market-driven form of Capitalism created by industrialization and intensified by the spread of information systems as the system evolved into globalization. In its present form, globalization requires extreme competition between countries for markets. Poor countries are at a disadvantage in that they have few commodities they can bring to the table to gain access into this global arena. When they find viable commodities to gain access to the global stage, they often run right into the brick walls of trade restrictions and barriers imposed by the developed world. For these countries, the more leisurely and less competitive version of Capitalism drawn from the time of agrarianism is preferable. In that system, they would have an easier time of moving into the global marketplace with their farm products. However, we cannot turn back the clock, so I am afraid their efforts to opt out of the global system will prove fruitless. The present form of Capitalism is too well-entrenched to be displaced. The system will continue to distribute surpluses of products and ideas despite the best efforts of some countries to withdraw from the system. In real terms, no single government can withdraw from the system, they can only force Capitalism to become an underground system as occurred in China and Russia during the early days of Communism. Where there is surplus, the natural system will come into play and establish itself to distribute that surplus. It is immaterial to the system of Capitalism whether this is done officially or unofficially; the system will continue to work.

The primary flaw in Capitalism, the stratification that occurs within the system, will be a problem for some time to come. As we saw in the early days of industrialization in England, there was a stratification of haves and have-nots. Governments modified this into a system of classes for their own purposes. In either case, the net result is the same: there will be people who are lacking in the skills necessary to compete effectively in the modern environment created by globalization/Capitalism. The government of India has perhaps hit upon the single most important factor for countries to be successful in this global environment: education. The creation of a viable educational system designed to take a portion of the population and to create within it the technical, scientific, and professional skills that the global marketplace requires is the only effective way to succeed. For countries such as India and Cuba, who have recognized that their schools can be a viable global commodity, they have been successful. In countries where this realization has not yet come into being, such as Africa, there has been less success. Capitalism has moved to the lowest common denominator: the human being. This was where we started at the very early stages of farming. Although industrialization moved our perceptions away from the individual, just as globalization has moved our perceptions away from individual countries, individuals within this system have a value, but that value is based upon the tools and capabilities they bring with them. The present form of Capitalism is a knowledge-based system. Those with the greatest skills and knowledge will have the most to trade. In the early days of farming, not every individual would be a successful farmer, yet there were individuals who were able to survive in this system because they brought other skills to the table.

Surplus enabled populations to develop different and diverse technologies. Many of these technologies would be useful and beneficial to holders of other types of surplus and promote and facilitate trade. The Internet as a system has created the ability for individuals to function as virtual sole-proprietorships and market their skills on a worldwide basis. A designer of websites in England can interface with a client in China, Russia, South America, the United States, or Africa. Today, an entrepreneur can operate a global business from any place in the world with minimal resources. The system of Capitalism is making each individual function as a business entity in the global marketplace. Individuals and countries that recognize this fact can benefit from it because the system is set up to facilitate that type of endeavor. As the system continues to function on a global basis, each individual will be responsible for bringing to the table tools, capabilities, or goods that the marketplace will value. The system of Capitalism has gone full circle, back to the individual as the functional element in the system.

Unintended Consequences of the System

The rapid expansion of economies had certain unintended consequences. The move from farming to industrialization took over 10,000 years. Industrialization occurred and was spread by Capitalism on a worldwide basis in less than 150 years. The final stage of Capitalism as a knowledge-based system occurred in just several decades. Countries had been able to move rapidly through a period of industrialization and into the information age. This expansion does not allow for societies to make careful and considered analyses of all the impacts of such rapid expansion. Governments need to supply jobs in order to keep their populations happy. People are not likely to wait decades for a country to carefully consider and work out all the ramifications of modernization; they move the process forward using the best available technology as quickly as possible. A prime commodity in this process is water. Water is an indispensable tool in modern societies. To understand this, let's take a look at some basic water facts.

If you ask people the importance of a barrel of oil in today's world, almost everyone can tell you how important energy is in the global marketplace. Yet ask the same individual about water and you will most likely get a blank stare. The simple truth is that we live on a planet composed of 75% water but where only 1% of all that water is available for human use. From that 1%, we must currently allocate 75% to agricultural needs of the world and 20% to industrial needs. This leaves a bare 5% of 1% for human consumption and sanitation. As the world's population has grown, the requirements for fresh water have increased 600% as referenced by Kofi Annan in *We the Peoples* (2000) published by the United Nations. It was this increase in demand for fresh water which prompted the United Nations through its United Nations Environmental Project, the World Bank, the International Monetary Fund, and a number of governments around the world, to begin an effort to protect this resource. Yet in today's world, the sad truth is that many governments find themselves without the economic ability to address this problem. Some are too poor or unstable, and others are more interested in military might than allocating appropriate resources to protecting critical water sources. Even in the United States, the government is moving toward privatization in areas that had traditionally been reserved as the sole responsibility of government. Privatization is a reality of today's world.

This move toward privatization of certain critical resources is necessary and proper. As governments find themselves unable to fulfill their obligations in certain key areas, it is necessary to turn to the private sector to generate resources to preserve the public good. However, private companies bring with them mixed blessings. It is not disputed that the primary driving force for most private organizations is profit. Yet until the face of the emergency can be placed in economic terms, the public will not recognize it as an emergency. When the price of oil was $10 a barrel, few people in this country or around the world recognized the problem of a growing population consuming from a fixed pool of resources. Now with oil prices above $75 a barrel, everyone recognizes the problem. So it is with water. There's a need to attach an economic face to the commodity before people will recognize its value and worth as a critical resource. Private companies fulfill that goal. As referenced in *Fortune* magazine in the article "Water, Water Everywhere" written by Shawn Tully in 2005, the financial stakes are tremendous. Water privatization represents a $400 billion a year industry. That is 40% the size of the oil sector. By placing it in these terms, we make it possible to attract private industry to the problem and we place it in perspective so that the average person can understand it in economic terms. The simple truth of the matter is that without help from private investment, much of the work needed to preserve fresh water will not be accomplished. Does this mean increasing prices for poor? The simple answer is "yes." But without privatization, the problem will not be resolved. That would be far more disastrous for everyone.

Currently it requires 450,000 gallons of water per year to meet the needs of the average person in the modern world. This amount is based on an allocation per person to meet the need for agriculture, industry, sanitation, and drinking. Falling below that level means becoming water-stressed. By 2025, two out of every three people on this planet will be living in areas that are water-stressed; they will not have enough water to survive, according to reports from the United Nations, the Global Water Project, the IMF, World Bank, and a host of other sources. To prevent this disaster, privatization is the only available answer.

According to the United Nations Environmental Project (UNEP), fresh water consumption has increased six fold from 1900 through 1995. Available and usable water supplies are becoming critical to global populations. Many countries such as Africa and West Asia are already in what the United Nations considers water-distressed areas. The following Illustration shows areas of water shortage globally.

Global Water Stress

1995

2025

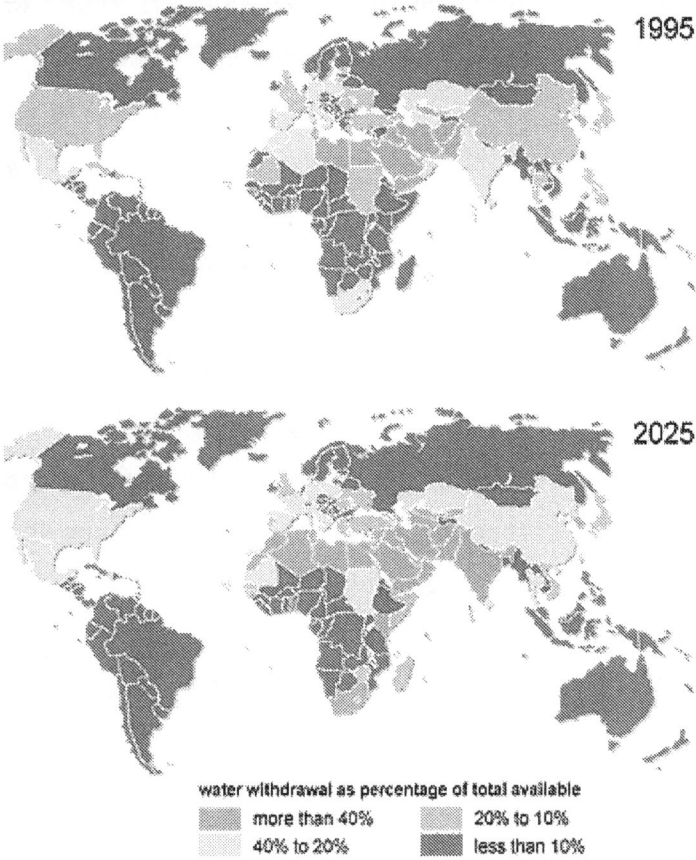

water withdrawal as percentage of total available

- more than 40%
- 40% to 20%
- 20% to 10%
- less than 10%

Note: water stress is defined as follows: low, less than 10% of total available is withdrawn moderate, 10-20% of total available is withdrawn medium-high, 20-40% of total available is withdrawn high, more than 40% of total available is withdrawn

From the United Nations Environmental Project website,GEO-2000outlook, http://www.unep.org/geo2000/english/0046.htm

Fully 20% of the world's population does not have access to safe drinking water. It is projected that by the year 2025, that 40% of the global population will be in water-deprived areas. This problem is often exacerbated by the rapid movement of countries through a small period of industrialization then rapidly into information-based technologies.

Technology consumes large quantities of fresh water. There's a growing competition between industrial facilities and human populations for this commodity. By moving so quickly through industrialization, many countries find themselves consuming water resources that cannot be replaced. In China, for instance, water consumption has increased almost 20% per year as the country has moved through industrialization and into the threshold of being an information-based society. Most of this increase is associated with industrial use. Manufacturing facilities and factories consume large quantities of water as these nations have attempted to move quickly into the global marketplace. The single largest consumer of fresh water still tends to be agriculture. With growing populations largely centered around urban areas of manufacture and production, agricultural regions have been forced to become more efficient. This often means relying upon the use of pesticides and fertilizers to achieve larger crop yields. The runoff from these chemicals as well as industrial wastes will often find its way into local water supplies. In China, is currently estimated that 70% of all the fresh water bodies in that country are contaminated. To put this into perspective, it is estimated that fully 40% of the Chinese population will consume water that is unsafe to drink on a daily basis.

India has its own water crisis. The world's second most populous nation has acute and chronic water shortages throughout much of the country. Just as in China, the rapid development of manufacturing facilities has created problems in terms of industrial wastes and competition with other critical areas such as farming. Africa tends to be one of the worsted continents because of recurring cycles of drought in much the sub-Saharan region. South America, also, has not escape unscathed in this process. Many countries within South and Central American are facing critical water shortages. Privatization of water resources within those regions has proved to be successful to a limited degree in providing relief. Privatization may be objectionable to many people, but it is the only source of revenue that can be brought to bear on this problem. The countries involved do not have the resources or, in many cases, the expertise to address the problems. By encouraging private companies who have both the resources and the expertise to become involved, international organizations are hoping to adequately address the problem. However, there is a growing backlash from many sectors concerning the privatization of water.

In many parts of the world, water is considered a communal resource, to be used, and often abused, by everyone. This concept has created great difficulty for local governments and their ability to adequately address the problem. If you tell people that a gallon of gasoline is going to increase from $1.75 a gallon to $3 a gallon because of supply problems, people can understand that, but try to explain to some people why a gallon of water will suddenly go from being free to costing them a substantial portion of their weekly income and you have a major problem. This is what happened in portions of South America during this past decade. The United Nations in conjunction with the International Monetary Fund and the World Bank made loans conditional on the privatization of water sources. In Chile, the process worked well. Private companies took control of the local water facilities and, within a period of a year, were able to correct many of the faults and produce clean and safe drinking water. This process was not without some cost, which resulted in many of the poor not being able to afford the clean, fresh water. The very people the process was intended to help were being denied the benefits.

Air pollution generated by countries moving rapidly through industrialization is also a problem. In 2005, there was an instance where Chinese facilities had spilled hazardous chemicals into a local water supply causing the evacuation of four million people. The problem did not stop there. The river into which the chemicals were spilled traveled north into

Russia, requiring additional evacuations of cities in that country. Similar situations have occurred in South America as countries have attracted industrial facilities only to see the waste from those facilities travel to neighboring countries and create problems. In that same way, air pollution is becoming a global concern. China is leading the way in that effort. China is currently the second biggest producer of greenhouse gases and, within a few short years, will become the global leader. In portions of China, pollution has become a significant factor prompting the Chinese government to undertake a program to correct the problem. It is slated to have a 15% reduction in their pollution within the next 25 years. Meanwhile, pollution from Chinese factories will often find its way to the American West Coast and into the skies above Los Angeles, Portland, Oregon, and Seattle, Washington. These factors will continue to have an impact on the human species as a whole.

As Capitalism has become increasingly driven by population pressures in its search for new marketplaces, these unintended consequences have profound impacts on both global stability and the habitability of the planet. It is perhaps these unintended consequences which are more significance than the actual operation of the system. It is impossible to tell six billion people that they will never be allowed to enjoy comparable lifestyles to Western societies. We cannot tell them that they will never be able to own an automobile, have a nice home, or to provide for their children a standard of living that they see emulated so often in commercials and movies from the West. Whether Humanity can balance these needs by moving large numbers of underdeveloped peoples into the global marketplace with these unintended consequences only time will tell.

As we move into the 21st century, it is clear that Capitalism will provide new challenges for humanity. The system will continue to facilitate the spread of technologies and ideas, which in some cases may provide stresses on human societies that we have never before seen. It is projected that China will have 500 million cars on the roads of that country with in the next 25 years. If there is a similar increase in India, South America, and Africa, will they be sustainable? We must look with clarity into the future of Capitalism in the face of growing population pressure. Is there an upper limit for the system beyond which stability may not be attainable? Global projections of the population show that it will reach ten billion by 2050. The impact of three billion more people seeking access to global markets and to standards of living based upon today's model may not be practical. There is always the argument to be made that technology will find a way to accommodate these people. Yet given the pressures exerted upon human culture by Capitalism and its need to balance the system, this appears to be problematic.

Beyond the purely theoretical, we must consider the purely practical. Water, energy, and food are the three most critical commodities for existence on this planet. To date, governments have made accommodations when these commodities were in short supply. Will that continue in the future? What happens in sub-Saharan Africa if continued cycles of drought accelerate and intensify? What will happen in China when there are three billion people in that country and the water supply is so contaminated that it cannot be used for human consumption? What will happen in India, which is quickly moving to pass China in terms of overall population, when water supplies create food shortages for that growing population? These are not just issues which affect Third World countries. In the United States in the Pacific Northwest, states have had to curtail further development in some areas because of a shortage of water. If the unintended circumstances continue, will we see further effort by governments to divide the world into the perpetual poor and the privileged wealthy?

Throughout history, we have seen many models where a few privileged individuals have attempted to control large numbers of poor and underprivileged people. In modern history, we can point to examples such as South Africa, Rhodesia, and the domination of India by Great Britain. In every case, control proved untenable. Are we looking at a comparable case in today's world in the distribution of technology and wealth between Western civilization and the developing world? Capitalism will not provide answers to these questions, but it will intensify our search for these answers as populations increase and the urgency for answers likewise increases. Capitalism has proved to be an effective natural system of the distribution of cultural information, products, and technologies, and in the final stages, ideas and knowledge. It is a robust system which has so far been able to defeat the intentions of Western civilizations to restrict the flow of certain information to under developed countries. Given this tendency, it is inevitable that at some point the system will eventually equalize itself and disseminate information and wealth, thereby equalizing all nodes within the system more or less uniformly. The final question, then, is: will it occur peacefully?

The Paradox of Nations

The concept of nations is an interesting one. How does a nation come into being? There are several theories about the formation of nations. Jared Diamond gave a good review of those theories in his book *Guns, Germs and Steel*. The first theory is Aristotle's which says that nations are a natural condition of human society. This is, of course, based upon Aristotle's view of the world of Greek societies in the fourth century B.C.E., making it a very narrow perspective that does not consider the rest of the world. The next theory is what is known as the "social contract theory," which was first put forward by Jean-Jacques Rousseau, the noted French philosopher. He speculated that nations are formed by a sort of rational transaction between citizens based upon their self-interest. People soon figured out they would be better in a large, organized group (the state) rather than being on their own. What Rousseau failed to see at the time was that in many cases, the small groups were forced, or coerced, into becoming part of the larger states. The third theory is what's known as the "hydraulic theory." This theory evolved as a way of explaining large irrigation projects in Mesopotamia, North China, Mexico, and Madagascar. In order for such large projects to be undertaken, there would be the need to create a central bureaucracy to direct activities. The problem with this theory is that the projects occurred after the formation of nations, and therefore did not accompany the emergence of states. Perhaps at this point, we should look not toward the historical model, but toward a new scientific model for the explanation of nations.

If we strip away the identifying characteristics and consider each individual or object in the system as a node and look simply at the connectivity between these nodes, we will begin to see the model proposed by Stephen Strogatz for synchronous systems. Once we do away with identifying characteristics and look at the complexity and connections of these nodes, we begin to see the pattern of a small world network emerge. It doesn't matter whether we're talking about brain cells, germs in a contagious disease, wildlife in the natural environment, the Internet, or groups of oscillators, it is the complexity of the connections between the nodes which is important. As we start discussing chaos theory and synchronicity, an unusual occurrence happens in small world networks of high complexity and connectivity called tipping. Tipping occurs when the connections in a system reach a certain point. The reason these connections exist in human networks often revolves around the concept of food. From the advent of farming, we can see that the creation of surplus food sources promoted connections between individual groups in the beginnings of trade. Some groups would have more food surplus than others, and some would not have a surplus of food at all but might have other commodities to trade which would involve different technologies such as weapons, clothing, architecture, arts, or any number of other endeavors. Natural systems would have occurred as interconnections were made between these disparate groups as they engaged in trade for items that they needed or desired. The interconnections created by these activities would hit a critical threshold where they would begin to accelerate and we would have a type of grouping occurring in the network called clomping. Clomping occurs because, at this level, the interconnections themselves have a significant impact on the network which is forming. The connections represent a significant new input and the system works to try to distribute that input throughout the network for equalization purposes. This type of activity has been seen in animal populations, fireflies, wildlife, mechanical systems dealing with oscillators, and highly technological systems such as the Internet; it occurs independently of whether it is a biological or non-biological system. Once this clomping begins, the interconnections will increase until they have reached another critical threshold, at which time they will slow down and eventually stop as the connections between the individual nodes in the system have little or no impact on the system itself. As food production increased, other forms of production increased, and population increased, we saw this process occurring many times within the system in the formation of larger, more complex groups of nodes centered around activities caused by their interconnections. The increasing complexities would force the system to begin self-organization to more effectively distribute surplus to the individual nodes. As the system would become larger, this process would become more complex, resulting in a greater need for self-organization to distribute surpluses within the complex structure. We must remember that simply because one complex structure is developing around farming (a desirable way of creating surplus food) it does not mean that other complex structures would not be developing around other methods of creating surplus. We would then have competing systems as Richard Dawkins explained in his book *The Selfish Gene*, which would then be in competition for survival. The competing systems would self-organize in order to create the greatest potential for survival. This organization around increasingly complex systems will eventually lead to the establishment of nations. The natural system would gradually begin to force self-organization for its own survival. This would mean creating structures to protect it from competing systems and to distribute surpluses more effectively within this system. A nation is nothing more than a group of individuals working together with some degree of self-interest. In the small world model, the self-interest is the survival of the system. Without the survival of the system, the result would be chaos. As groups began to recognize this self-interest, the system moved toward self-organizing groups beyond the tribe and the city to eventually become nations organized around the self-interest of the system: the system's survival through the creation of surplus. The ultimate goal of the system was to create surplus because surplus made it possible for a number of things to occur which were favorable: cultural exchanges in the form of different technologies and trades, the evolution and development of new technologies and trades, and individuals having time to pursue endeavors aside from gathering food. This again resulted in population pressures and started a new cycle of interconnectivity, which would lead to another tipping point. We now begin to see how nations might evolve based upon an analysis of complex systems without regard to characteristics of the individual nodes. Once the system reached a certain size, organization would become imperative in order for the system to survive.

Despite the natural formation of social structure as a result of complex interconnectivities, we must not look at the system as if it existed within a vacuum. There are many such small world models in existence, competing at different levels, such as the human brain and infectious diseases. Once any of these systems has reached a certain level of complexity, self-organization begins to occur within the individual nodes, which now make up the system. Social structure within each node would begin to take on a complexity and self-organizing structure just as complex as the larger system to which it was connected. At a certain point, the nodes become large enough that they would create complexity within themselves independent of the larger system in which they were operating. The complexity within the nodes then became distinct from Capitalism and, in some cases, at odds with the system.

Just as the human body is a conglomeration of systems that sometimes work in harmony with each other and sometimes will be at odds with each other resulting in system collapse, so the system of Capitalism became a conglomeration of systems that sometimes do and sometimes do not work well. The social systems which have evolved within the individual nation nodes have often placed themselves in conflict with the larger system of Capitalism. The needs of individual social clusters, or nations, often create obstructions to the natural flow of the system. Nations have evolved as social networks designed to control human behavior. They have a drive for self-preservation just as the system of Capitalism does. However, where one seeks to distribute surplus uniformly throughout all of the nodes, social constructs, or nations, the other seeks to preserve itself by restricting the free flow of surplus throughout the system. As we discussed earlier, this sometimes takes the form of trade restrictions or trade prohibitions. It is interesting that the natural evolution of Capitalism has created such a wonderful complexity with in the complexity of the system. Nations become systems of complexity revolving around the individual states and cities within the nation. The cities and states become systems of complexity revolving around groups of geographical divisions within them. This process cycles down from one level of complexity to another until we reach an individual within a particular nation and continue past that point to the individual as a system composed of the human brain and the human cell. What we have in truth is a Mandelbrot set showing complexity extending into infinity. Nations are a simple part of that complexity.

Yet by looking at the system in terms of its interconnections between nodes, we can begin to explore it more fully and completely. Synchronicity then provides the final part as we look at self-organization of nodes. This principle is part of the evolving field which looks at natural systems of complex connectivity evolving out of chaos. From a systems standpoint, we can begin to understand how a simple stock to the system, in this case surplus food, can move it to expand in terms of complexity and to reorganize itself into a comprehensive system that we call Capitalism. It provides an explanation for the formation of tribes, chiefdoms, kingdoms, and finally nations as the system has moved through various stages of absorbing new impacts and shocks that it has attempted to distribute uniformly throughout the system. Within the system, we can see other levels of complexity created by social interaction, which sometimes are at odds with the overall system. It is a picture of a Mandelbrot type set, moving through cycles of complexity from the very large to the infinitely small by use of this simple replication process. It is ironic that nations are often at war with the very system that created them.

Nations represent an interesting paradox. Created from the natural evolution of the Capitalist system and evolved for the purpose of controlling people and things, they are part of an intricate network which promotes the distribution of people and things for system equalization. The growing conflict between the nations as a social system and the overall system of Capitalism will provide many years of discussion and analysis for all areas of science. In the social arena, we will see the continuous evolution of conflicts between social systems in Western countries. A counterbalancing system is evolving in countries such as India and China as well as the countries of Africa and South America. The international model, as I term it, places a great deal of emphasis upon the natural system as opposed to social systems. There's been a great deal of discussion about the viability of many of these social systems in the global markets of today. Globalization has placed a great deal of pressure upon Western economies to become more like the international community and to abandon many of their social requirements. There is a great deal of resistance to this within the communities of the Western world. This creates the conflict between the global system of Capitalism and nations.

Should any single nation or group of nations be able to dictate to a majority of the world populations how to run their economies? Will the nations of the world finally agree on the importance of establishing consensus guidelines and rules which will govern all players in the system fairly? These are just two of the critical questions which must be answered as we move into the future as part of this large system we call

Capitalism. Having understood how it evolved from the modest roots of farming to be the complex system that exists today does not create a road map for us as to what it will be tomorrow. There will be other significant developments that will create shocks to the system, forcing it to evolve to new levels. We have no idea what those shocks may be, only that they will occur. The stratification which exists in Capitalism will always be a problem, and we have no way of determining if new kicks to the system will further intensify stratification or will in some way mitigate it. What we do know is that the system has survived for many thousands of years and continues to survive in a very healthy and rigorous format today. It is unlikely that it will stop its evolution at this point. The larger questions become whether the conflict with nations will result in a disruption of the system which will ultimately cause systemization or whether this conflict between competing systems will continue without having a significant impact.

As was stated before, human civilization needs Capitalism. We have become so intertwined with this system that it is inconceivable to think of human existence without it. The very fact that it has spread so prolifically all around the world to every corner of civilization is a testament to its ability to provide advantages to those groups who embrace it. The system embodied by Capitalism (surplus, market, and profit) has helped move humanity from an agrarian society into a modern space-fairing technology. To say that there are not been debits to the system would be to ignore the obvious. However, the pros far outweigh the cons. As we move into the 21st century, the massive system which encompasses our globe in the universe, Earth, will continues to evolve as the planet itself evolves. We will all have to wait and see exactly where that evolution will lead us.

Our perception of Capitalism must change if we are to be effective in understanding this system. We have tended to look at our world and Capitalism as two entities related in a certain way. Perhaps some imagery is in order. Let us think of humanity as being large land masses and Capitalism as being the rivers flowing through and connecting us together economically, culturally, or socially. That has been the analogy we have used in constructing the ways we deal with the global system to date. I think a more apt analogy is humanity represented as a series of islands located in an ocean and that ocean is named Capitalism. The natural system which has evolved around humanity is independent of human beings. The first analogy makes it possible for us to believe that we can control the way Capitalism works in much the same way we would control the river. We could construct ways of redirecting its flow and harnessing its energies by systems of controls, or dams, placed in the proper locations. This gives us a feeling of security as humans because we are in control. In reality, humanity resembles more the image of islands in a very broad and complex ocean. The interconnections that we have constructed over many generations connect us across this ocean in a number of different ways, but it is the ocean which is in control, not the islands. The tools and methods we use to survive as islanders are very different from those we would employ living on a continent. Islanders are much more susceptible to the whims of the forces around them. They understand that their ability to control such forces is often limited. They continue their existence one step away from falling prey to larger forces such as storms, earthquakes, and potential tsunamis. Many of these forces are beyond the direct control of the people who live on the island. However, survival dictates that they become aware of these forces so that they may eventually plan for the occurrence, so must modern societies began to plan for disasters created by the natural system.

This becomes important because globalization has increased the rate at which developing countries are industrializing. This rapid increase in activity consumes quantities of natural resources that cannot be replaced easily and creates the unintended consequence of pollution which affect all members of the global population. It is often too easy to think that we can simply put in place a series of regulations to solve a problem which extends beyond humanity. Unintended consequences cannot be so easily handled. When over three-fourths of the world's population is struggling to provide a modest standard of living for themselves, it is unlikely they will stop the industrialization and what this engenders simply because the developed countries find it inconvenient. Unfortunately, the result of these efforts may be detrimental to everyone. It is only when we understand that we are part of a larger system that we can clearly begin to see the need to create census agreements which work for the common good of the global population. Without such agreements in place, each country will act with degrees of independence which will create problems that the whole world must deal with in terms of water shortages and global pollution and its resultant impact on global climates. The increasing competition between the emerging developing countries and developed countries for critical resources must be brought under control or the system itself will become critically unstable. We must find ways to accommodate emerging nations and to bring them successfully into the global marketplace while at the same time minimizing the unintended consequences which they often bring with them in rapid industrialization.

As Kenneth Jowett points out in his book *The New World Order*, we have grown confused, mistaking order for the concept of being in control. The movement of globalization to break down barriers and to redistribute ideas, product, and technology on a global basis shatters this illusion. It leaves us with the feeling that the world is suddenly in chaos. This is nothing more than realization that the nation's states are going the way of the dinosaurs and global systems are dominating.

The spread of free trade, as facilitated by globalization, has resulted in the free movement of capital. Control of capital is a central pillar of the nation-states extension of political necessity. Nations have often attempted to control the flow of money as a means of regulating Capitalism. It has proved a futile effort.

When Capitalism first became self-organizing in the early days of farming, there were no nation-states in existence. The system worked in conjunction with humanity as farming spread from the Fertile Crescent to Asia and Africa and beyond. It was unfettered and uncontrolled. For over 10,000 years, the system worked with humanity to disseminate and redistribute surplus technologies, cultural ideas, materials, and wealth throughout the agrarian communities of humanity. There were many small and independent spheres of influence in existence at that time, identified as kingdoms, tribes, or chiefdoms as reference by Jared Diamond in his book, *Guns, Germs, and Steel*. These groupings posed little resistance to Capitalism and there was a continuous and easy spread of cultural information, or memes, for a long period of time. It was not until we reach the modern age with the rise of nation-states that we begin to see disruptions in the system and the consolidation of human power into nation-states in attempts to control Capitalism. The Adam Smith model created in the 1700s at the start of industrialization, promoted the concept that nations must control the flow of goods and services within and without its boundaries in order to be successful. As a result of that model, the recognized centers of power in the world consolidated effectively to approximately 12: China, Japan, the individual nation-states of Europe, and the colonies of America, South America, and India. With new abilities to control production and transportation of surplus, these nation-states began to exert control with catastrophic results by the time we reach the early portion of the 19th century.

Despite these efforts, the system continued to survive and to break down barriers, so that by the time we reach the middle of the 20th century, we have reduced the influence of nation-states to three spheres of influence: the Western democracies, the Communist countries, and independent nation-states. As the nation-states have begun to recognize their impotence in the face of this natural system, we've begun to see further deterioration of national centers of influence to one in today's modern world: the United States. I know there will be people who will point to the European Union and the rise of Communist China and India as spheres of influence, but they are developing spheres, largely constrained by the forces of Capitalism. The United States is the preeminent nation-state in existence in the world today. Its ability to effect changes within the structure of Capitalism has been giving way to the growing need to establish consensus within the international community. The need to create consensus agreements with the full participation of all countries and all people has become the only viable model for moving forward successfully in the 21st century.

Capitalism in the global context has begun to reduce and eliminate barriers until there are none left, placing the burden of competition squarely upon the shoulders of each individual within the collective system to be responsible for their own present and future. We have become a collection of nodes within a giant system which requires that each individual function as if it were a corporate entity responsible for creating, maintaining, and marketing assets and engaging in the necessary exchange between nodes, cultures, and nations. Rapid expansion of communications and technology makes it possible for each individual to establish and create many connections within this global system of the kind that can reach beyond national boundaries. Until we recognize the truth of this concept, we cannot begin to understand the true nature of Capitalism and how we may effectively coexist with it and profit from the operations of the system. As tiny islands interconnected in a great ocean, it is the interconnections between the individual nodes, or people, which are important. We can understand the behavior of the intricate and complicated nature of the giant system of which we are part, but we are powerless to control it. There are tenants of the system we can identify and examine in detail. This will give us insight and understanding of how the relationship with the system will and must evolve.

The heart and soul of the nation-state is education. An educational system can determine how effectively and successfully an individual nation will be in the modern world. This is the great strength of nations and perhaps their greatest weakness. In the early development of mankind, organized education came from three distinct areas: the military, the church, and labor guilds.

The rise of organized militaries has been in continuous evolution since the very early stages of human existence. The creation of military units and their organization was of critical importance in stabilizing and controlling surplus. There was little purpose in growing food if it was to be taken away from you immediately and given to someone else. In this regard, the creation of military forces was essential to protect surplus even in the age of agrarianism. As humanity progressed into city-states, kingdoms, and eventually nations, this concept of the military as a necessary tool evolved as well.

Another major institution concerned with education was the church. Religious organizations often founded schools to train the next generation to carry on their religious teachings. This would often entail various degrees of technological advancement. The earliest scribes came from religious organizations. Much of the historical record of early human development comes from religious writings.

The final group, the labor guilds, came into being as specialized professionals in the trades. They were largely responsible for creating and maintaining the quality of their individual professions and acting as a screening mechanism to keep out un-qualified persons.

The interesting thing about each of these groups is that they were primarily designed to exclude people and to restrict the flow of information. These human creations were opposed to the natural flow of Capitalism. In the earliest days, because human groups were scattered and poorly organized, they represented little of an impediment to the dissemination of memes, which are critical to the survival of the natural system. As these human-created systems became more numerous and well-developed, they began to entrench the concept of control of technology and information into their governing structures. Adam Smith was one of the first to place this concept in writing when he described mercantilism. Nations must restrict and control the flow of material and information within and without their borders. This need for restrictions served nations very well in the beginning. As cities evolved into nation-states, they saw the practical use of formal education as not only a way to educate and maintain a sufficient labor class, but as a political tool for indoctrination and control. Educational systems were a way of ensuring the loyalty of populations to the state. In every nation, a form of a pledge of allegiance to the state is required in the education system.

In each of the systems we just talked about (the military, the church, and labor guilds) the fundamental principle is to control and restrict information and the types of people allowed access to that information. This is at the heart of the education system as it exists today in the modern world. Each country creates an educational system which works within strictly controlled parameters designed to further the political goals of an individual nation. This creates a sort of educational box within which only certain kinds of information are disseminated. Some information is deemed beneficial to the state and will be allowed mass dissemination; other information is detrimental and will be prohibited. We've seen these types of prohibitions come into play throughout human history. There have been prohibitions against certain types of religions and certainly prohibitions against military education which seeks a different path than that of the established state. Trade unions often placed restrictions on their members to ensure quality and competence of the profession. By restricting the type and manner of the dissemination of information, we limited our perspectives of the world as we know it.

Thomas S. Kuhn was a noted historian of science who first recognized this principle as it applied to scientific learning. He pointed out that much of science is nothing more than a tidying up in well-established areas and maintaining a rigid status quo. The true learning and expansion of scientific knowledge comes from the abrupt departure from the status quo caused by what he describes as revolutions that separate us from learned methods and force us into new learning paradigms. With every significant evolution in scientific thought and the development of new theories, there were people who were ostracized and driven from the mainstream, but who had the strength of conviction to continue their work and to force enlightenment onto the larger scientific community. This process happens on an infrequent and irregular basis throughout history. This is also the same way in which educational systems in general function and expand. The first purpose of the conventional educational system is not to engender new research but to protect and maintain the established research principles and theories. This often means excluding things which were not part of the accepted norm and actively engaging in preventing the dissemination of information which does not meet accepted standards. This means that on many occasions, societies, who were depended upon these educational systems to move them forward and to help them prepare for future difficulties and problems, were left with a perspective of the world that does not often show reality. They created a static vision which kept them from seeing new and unusual potential dangers and changes as they were about to occur. As an example of this, we need only look at the world of medical science which, until the 18th century, maintained the belief that women had one more rib in their anatomy than men. There are thousands of similar stories concerning not only medicine and science, but all of human social systems. We have tended to allow education to color the world in terms that are politically correct for the nation, and sometimes the picture does not allow us to see dangers until it is too late.

This same promise was put forward in part by Jared Diamond in his recently released book *Collapse: How Societies Choose to Fail or Succeed*. In what he terms "reasoning by false analogy," he points to the problem in which individual societies create false images and perpetuate them to their own detriment. This is largely done through an educational system which is designed to promote and protect state interest and not to expand human knowledge. The evolution of chaos theory was one such example. The possibility of order existing in the perturbations of massive irregular systems all round us was largely ignored because it was simpler to study the cleaner and neater linear systems which had nice concise solutions. It was only due to the diligence of a handful of dedicated scientists and individuals, we're able to push forward the barriers of human knowledge and expand our sense of understanding of the larger world around us. This characteristic flaw of existing educational systems creates a problem in understanding our relationship to large, complex, natural systems and how they will affect us both in the short-term and long-term. As long as nations maintain educational systems for the purpose of maintaining national status quo, we will create an educated populace that is unable to see the world in its true form. Education must become a tool for the expansion of human knowledge and not for political purposes.

As we push forward the borders of human understanding, we serve all of humanity by gaining a greater knowledge of the systems which encompass us as human beings in our global environment. It is only through this process that we will be able to take off the blinders which can often lead us down a road to societal collapse. In this sense, it is this traditional mode of education which creates much of the unintended damage that we see caused by Capitalism. Nations put their own interest before anything else. They justify this under a series of reasons, which all boil down to one central explanation: the nation wishes to survive on its own terms. This means that countries will often attempt to exclude other countries from knowledge and cultural information because they believe it is in their nation's best interest, although it may not be in the best interests of the global environment. Other nations will sacrifice people and culture in an effort to duplicate the most successful model on the planet, Capitalism, without regard the long-term consequences to their populations or to the world. Until we move ourselves and our education systems beyond the restrictions of political correctness and focus them on the true goal of expanding human knowledge, we will not have an education system that will give humanity a fighting chance to see potential problems before they become disasters.

It is often the most unusual of unintended consequences that can be most problematic. As strong central governments began to proliferate around the planet, social agendas came into play. Social agendas are based upon the cultural and historical aspects of the individual nation involved. Recently, the social aspects have begun to create friction with the natural system of Capitalism. Historically, the strong central government has been at odds with this natural system since the early 1700s. Adam Smith sounded the national anthem of this conflict in his book *The Wealth of Nations*. The concept that nations needed to garner wealth within their borders and to contain it there has become a central tenet of most national governments. Likewise, societies within these nations have ingrained within themselves the concept of social priorities, , which means that a nation will ignore the larger system of Capitalism and focus on a particular social agenda which promotes a false sense of reality. In the United States and Europe, this often causes resistance to any changes within the social fabric that goes against the grain of these perceptions. It has been assumed in the Western world that a certain standard of living would not only be maintained, but would continue to increase as the economic benefit created by continuing economic growth spread into the future. This concept is usually interpreted to indicate a growing middle-class group within these societies that would continue to expand and to enjoy wealth at a certain level as defined by that society. This more often than not meant high wages with the expectation of continuing increases into the foreseeable future. Globalization, as it spread Capitalism all round the world, comes into conflict with that concept.

Globalization and the natural system of Capitalism which drives globalization create stratification within society. With the movement of ideas, products, and technologies throughout the global systems, there is a realignment of economic realities in favor of the majority global population. As this process takes place, economic status becomes defined in a global context and not in any national context. This means that we move into a period of time where market forces are determined globally. A worker in any category will no longer be able to measure his or her worth based upon his or her position within a specific country, but must look at the global market to determine his or her worth. This new reality means that people in some countries, particularly in the Western world, who have enjoyed exceptionally high standards of living for a very long period of time, may now find themselves in a position of declining wages. This has nothing to do with economic prosperity of their country but with the new reality of a global marketplace rather than a national market place.

One example of this principle can be seen when we look at certain Western companies such as Caterpillar. For a long period of time, companies such as Caterpillar were the mainstay for unions since they promising stable employment and high wages for certain skill positions. Recently, the United Auto Workers, the principal union involved with Caterpillar, was forced to realize that it was no longer possible to insist upon wages based upon an American scale but now had to base the wages for its union members on a new global scale. During a period of negotiations, Caterpillar was forced to reduce the payment for skill positions from $50 an hour plus an additional 30% in benefits, to a new value of $25 an hour plus an additional $6 to $7 an hour for benefits. This new value was based upon global pay scales rather than United States pays scales. Caterpillar is not the only company forced to make such adjustments. More recently, General Motors and Ford Motor Company have begun a series of realignments and layoffs to bring their pay scale and debt structure into line with global norms. This forced realignment creates stratification in that it places more people outside of the normal range of middle-class status. Globalization creates jobs, but in reality, those jobs may not be created in the economically prosperous Western world but more often in the emerging countries of the developing world. Along with the creation of these jobs is a necessary downward movement of pay scales to accommodate the entry of new workers from these countries into the market. Their pay scales are lower than Western pay scales and will remain at that level for some time to come. This resulting counter-pressure forces wages within Western countries downward as well. It might seem at first glance that this would be an undesirable result for many of the Western countries since it results in the displacement of many who have been middle-class, or seek middle-class status, into a lower tier of the economic structure. However, at the same time, it will result in net movement of hundreds of millions of people from the very lowest levels of economic status in the developing world into a new middle-class status as defined by global standards. This may be of little consolation to the worker in Detroit or Ohio who loses the $50 an hour job, but in the global context, it is a net gain for the global society. As these changes take place, we may begin to see conflict erupt as nations take issue with the changes that globalization forces upon them.

The changes are not necessarily all economic, although economic changes are a significant and very important part of the unintended consequences of globalization. As we started this discussion, we were looking primarily at societal changes that are forced by globalization. In that context, economic changes create societal changes, but it is more importantly the exchange of cultures, ideas, and people which promotes the greatest changes wrought by globalization. The family that has lived in the Midwest or in the Northeast United States for generations, wrapped in the comfortable cocoon of familiar faces and cultures, will often find themselves in a very different environment as globalization proceeds. Communities that were once homogeneous, will now become increasingly diverse. Just as this disruption caused by rapid change and unfamiliar surroundings can create chaos within communities, so to can it create chaos within countries.

Recently in the United States, there was a great deal of anger and resentment engendered when a proposed Arab country, the United Arab Emirates, was slated to take over operation of portions of six U.S. ports. Government and citizens were inflamed and outraged that this would be allowed. After many weeks of protest and recriminations, the proposed takeover was halted. Although it was pointed out that most of the ports operated with the United States are operated by companies from foreign countries, this was little solace to the government or the citizens of the United States. The population demanded that such facilities be operated by Americans for national security reasons. When this situation is looked at without the emotional component, we can see that the request being made is unreasonable in light of globalization. Globalization fosters competition and creates a situation where larger is better. As competition increases, profit margins become smaller. An American company operating a single port will not be able to survive on the profit margins that exists for port operators in the United States or in much of the rest of the world. The only companies that can survive on those small margins are companies that have a very large global footprint, operating in multiple facilities all around the globe. Such large companies are able to survive on the small margins because they have many facilities. There is an analogy that makes this clear. If you are a manufacturer of plates with a profit margin of half a cent per plate and you only produce ten thousand plates a year, you will soon be out of business. If, on the other hand, you are a manufacturer of plates with a profit margin of half a cent per plate and you produce ten million plates per day on a global basis, you have profitability and can survive. The reality of port operations is very much the same. By operating a large number of facilities all around the globe, international companies can survive on small profit margins because of the economy of scale. Most of the large international companies tend to be foreign companies and not American companies, a fact that was lost in the emotional turmoil of the moment. Globalization creates and fosters the need for economies of scale. Larger companies can survive in the environment of extreme competition because the economies of scale can make them profitable.

It was not just the issue of ports and international companies which make the social unintended consequences of globalization so clear in today's world. At the same time that the emotional issue of national security based upon the control of seaports was being argued in United States, the chief economic rival of the United States was having a similar argument for the very same reasons. The National Assembly for the Chinese government was meeting during this same period of time, confronted with a resurgence of old line communists who were insisting there was a need to slow down Capitalism and to revisit the principles of socialism in that country. The resultant economic growth in China had created stratification. While there were economic centers of prosperity in many regions of the country, usually located around coastal regions or seaports, much of the interior of the country remained poor. There is a growing degree of unrest within China. The economic prosperity which is blossoming throughout the country is not moving into the rural countryside where the majority of the people live. As a result of this stratification, there is a growing division between haves and have-nots and a resurgence of hard-line officials arguing that social change should be stopped and that China should be moving back toward socialism. This argument came to a head in China as the National Assembly was beginning to discuss the critical issue of property rights for all its citizens. The fundamental concept of business in the global environment is the ownership of property. It has long been a criticism of China that property rights were not adequately protected in that country. Just as the country was beginning to move toward insuring this protection, the stratification caused by globalization engendered an emotional response to protect ingrained social systems within that country. It is too early to tell at this point if the hard-liners will make any serious inroads in reversing China's economic growth, but the battle is well under way. It is not just China and United States that has to deal with this social issue, it is something that is spreading to the entire world.

Concurrently with these events in China and the United

States, France was finding itself deeply embroiled in street riots and violence in Paris. Cars were burnt and shop windows were destroyed within blocks of the Eiffel Tower. Massive protests had been held not only in Paris but throughout many portions of France over the last several weeks because of the government's proposed change in employment law. The French government wants to make it possible for employers to hire and fire younger workers more easily. This would then encourage employers to hire more young workers. Currently in French law, it is very difficult to fire a young worker without having to go through the lengthy and often expensive process. To fire a young worker in France can often cost an employer more money than simply keeping the worker on until they leave of their own accord. There are currently four ways to fire a worker in France. A company can try to prove that the position needs to be abolished is not economically feasible. This can require a complex economic social plan which must show why the job cannot be transferred or the worker retrained. The second option is to prove the worker has done something wrong, which can also result in lengthy and costly litigation. Third, a worker can be paid to leave. This process can be extremely expensive as it usually includes months of severance pay, notice pay, and damages. Finally, employers are left with the least economic choice of putting the worker in a harmless position and waiting for them to quit out of boredom, resentment, or lack of incentives to stay. This is called "putting them in the cupboard." This oddity in French law has made it undesirable for many employers to hire young workers because they are so hard to fire. As a result, the unemployment among younger workers in France is running above 7%. Despite this fact, when the government announced its intentions to change the law, the youth of France took to the streets in massive numbers to protest the action. A part of this has to do with French culture but a large portion of it has to do with concepts being ingrained into French society based upon a different economic time and reality. Just as union workers resists change within the United States and hard-liners resist change in China because of past realities, the young people of France were resisting change based upon the past realities rather than the present or future realities of globalization. As of the writing of this portion of the text, the riots in France were still ongoing.

This is the major issue confronting globalization and the natural system of Capitalism which promotes globalization. Social changes resulting from globalization will cause nations to resist it because it means a change from expected benefits to the realities of what is available. Often the stratification engendered will be at odds with the neatly framed social categories that nations foster and encourage people to believe in. In the world of globalization, there are two crude categories as opposed to the three categories envision in the Western model created by Adam Smith. Instead of having three categories of wealthy, middle-class, and poor, there are two very crude groups of haves and have-nots. These groups represent less of an economic reality than they do a simple system reality: Capitalism's needs to create a balance by moving surplus through exchange to where it is needed. One group creates the surplus that the system seeks to redistribute. In the global system, conditions are fluid and may change over time as the system dictates. This critical exchange is often made more difficult by nations where there is insistence that a particular nation must have a particular economic reality. It is too early to tell which will prevail, whether nations will be successful in preventing the free flow of information or if the system will continue to diminish the importance of nations and foster the further spread of information freely.

Another unintended consequence of globalization occurs because of its connectivity. Once connections are made between the individual nodes of the system, they cannot be undone. This principle was first articulated by student in a class I was teaching during 2005 entitled, "Wealth and Power in America" in Seattle. One of the students in the class during the discussion about industrialization pointed out that when connections are made between entities or people, they tend to be permanent. No matter how we may wish to remove the connection, it cannot be done. We can alter or even attempt to limit the information transmitted through the connection, but we cannot undo it. This principle of Capitalism creates a particular problem in today's world. As the world grows more interconnected, it facilitates the transmission of not only products, but ideas, technology, and information generally. The system needs this transmission in order to sustain its existence. Unfortunately, once connections are made and the process of interchange has begun, the system has no way of defining how the transmission of information is to be used; it simply facilitates the exchange.

Oftentimes, countries will seek to interrupt these connections and the exchange of information, technologies, and products for various purposes as we saw with the Soviet Union and China. In all cases, these efforts proved futile. The United States is the latest of a series of nations undertaking to limit and to control the exchange portion of Capitalism. These efforts are largely because of a single entity: terrorism. The information age has created a free flow of information and technology which is unparalleled in history. This information moves freely throughout the global network and is available to any party with the resources and technology to access it. This often means that people whose interests are adverse to national stability for whatever reason can also gain access to this information. Since the attack on the American society on September 11th, 2001, The United States of America has been engaged in a war against terrorism. In most cases, the term "terrorist" is a misnomer. In every society, there have been factions who oppose the status quo and seek change for their own reasons. These entities are often the first to use violence as a means of instituting change since they do not have access to resources or political systems to affect change otherwise.

As the field of globalization has become more accessible to developing countries, many of these factions have found the information made available by the global system of information dispersal an attractive means of furthering their goals. The world has truly become flat, as Thomas L. Friedman indicated in his national best seller, *The World Is Flat* about the expansion of technology and global systems in the 21st century. As technology has made life easier for people in the developed world, it is also old created an exchange of information and technology with the developing countries as part of the ongoing interchange created by the natural system of Capitalism. The result of this is information moves more freely around the global and is accessible to large numbers of people. The number of factions which have come into existence in the 21st century possibly exceed the number in existence at any other time in world history. These individual factions tend to be more violent, better funded, better organized, and more technologically astute in the use of the global information network to achieve their ends. For every political faction which has come into existence, whether from Palestinian organizations or other places in the world, use of global communications has proved invaluable. In many portions of the Middle East, because of ongoing warfare, the institutions on which society depends to control and limit these individual factions are nonexistent. As we saw with the Taliban in Afghanistan, when societal systems break down, factions may rise to levels of supreme power within an individual region. Once this occurs, it may become difficult to dislodge them short of an application of force.

However, not all factions are bad. While many may espouse violence, there are many thousands of others which promote the necessary change and enlargements of the pool of human knowledge. It is the inability of the system to determine good from bad among these groups which causes the problem. In truth, the system has no concept of good or evil; it simply understands the fundamental principles necessary for its survival. In order to continue, the system must distribute surplus product, information, technology, or culture wherever there is a need. This system simply functions based upon its three governing principles to continue its existence. This inability of the natural system to make differentiation between what is good for society and what is bad is a primary cause for nations to resist the operation of the system in many regards. Despite this truth, the system will continue to do what it is necessary to maintain and to propagate itself. We begin to see in real terms that the conflict between societies created by human nations and the natural system which has evolved around those nations, Capitalism, have differences that bring them into conflict with each other. Sometimes those conflicts go to the very core of the survival of each. Nations thrive on control and enforcement of order within their borders. In order to ensure this, it is often necessary to place restraints upon factions whose political motivations may be disruptive. The natural system of Capitalism has no such concern; it simply wants to maintain the three fundamental drives critical to its survival. It will create surplus, exchange that surplus within its network in an effort to balance itself, and achieve the benefit of continued survival and expansion. Only time will tell if these differences can be accommodated so that both systems may survive.

As globalization continues with its own evolution, new and unique problems become more evident. As we have talked earlier, we recognized immigration as one of the seminal problems to be faced in globalization. It is a problem, however, with a double-edged sword. The evolution of Capitalism, or globalization, into an information technology system has, for the first time, made it possible to use technology in ways never anticipated before. This system of Capitalism, which engenders globalization, is making it possible for technology to affect our world in many different ways. The problem of immigration, although not unique to the United States, has proved a very turbulent and emotional issue for the American public. Each year, millions from South America, Central America, and Mexico cross the border to the United States seeking employment. Each time this issue is addressed, politicians and much of the American public seem confused and bewildered as to why people would leave their homes, families, and friends to come to America and work in low-paying, menial jobs. Part of the problem is the responsibility of the United States, but it is not because there is a higher standard of living in the United States than there is in Mexico.

If we look around the globe, we will see numerous instances where countries with large populations living in relative poverty do not flow across the borders with their neighbors in large numbers. The major problem between the United States and the countries of Latin America is one of an imbalance in trade relations. The United States is a country with the huge surpluses of technology and wealth. Capitalism seeks to move that surplus in an orderly fashion to where it is most needed. This process often takes the form of American corporations who proceeded to Mexico and to much of Latin America to find cheap labor sources and cheap sources of raw materials. As American and Western corporations seek to exploit these new markets in an effort to maximize profitability, they create wealth within certain urban areas of Latin America and extreme poverty within the rural country side. Most American corporations place their facilities near large urban centers, or cities. These act as an attractive magnet, siphoning away from the countryside and from the agricultural sector large numbers of skilled workers to better-paying manufacturing jobs. However, there are never enough of these jobs to satisfy the demand. As a result, the country winds up with a significant number of unemployed people in the cities and a growing number of farming communities which no longer are tenable. This is further exacerbated by the policy of the United States government toward Latin American countries. It uses them as a convenient market for subsidized agricultural products.

In today's world, Latin-American countries such as Mexico have become captive markets to American agribusiness. Mexico already has a staggering $2 billion debt with the United States because of the farm trade. With the application of NAFTA, this debt will continue to mount until 2008 when tariffs are removed, then it will skyrocket as American agribusiness will dump American government-subsidized farm products into the Mexican market. Already production of wheat in Mexico has fallen by 60% since 1980 and soybean production by one third. The numbers will be increased as the tariffs which were imposed by the Mexican government will be lifted and the United States agricultural business entities will unleashed a torrent of genetically-engineered and cheap products into the Mexican market. Currently, Mexico protects its critical agricultural product, corn, under protective tariffs to prevent such encroachment by U.S. companies. Once these protections are lifted, the central pillar of Mexican farming will be under attack from cheaper American farm products. Tom Thompson, a specialist in unfair trade practices, pointed out that it costs three times as much to ship the farm products by rail from Sinaloa to Mexico City as it does to ship it from New Orleans to Veracruz. As prices for petroleum increase, the difference in costs will increase.

We sometimes tend to forget that despite its size, Mexico is still predominantly an agricultural nation. Yet in today's world, such nations can become, and often are, target markets because of technology. America is the world's largest supplier of genetically-engineered agricultural seeds. These seeds are critical to agricultural countries, yet they are costly to buy. In an effort to reduce cost, Mexican and many third world farmers have reverted to the age-old method of saving part of each year's harvest to use as seed stock for the next year, thus reducing cost. This also reduces the amount of sales from American agribusiness, something corporations already starved for profit cannot accept. Most recently, the Department of Agriculture instituted a new program with an American research firm to insure that seeds sold to other countries can only be used for one planting. The seeds are genetically designed so that once they are planted, the plants are programmed to produce only sterile seeds. This means that farmers must buy new quantities of seeds each year in order to plant new crops. Mexico is an importer of agricultural seeds from the United States. This means that the central pillar of Mexico, its farming community, will be held hostage to genetic engineering from the United States. A country which is already steeped in poverty will become even poorer as it is forced to buy expensive genetically-engineered seeds from American companies each year. Mexico could choose to fight legal battles against the companies which create the seeds, but to fight a patent infringement battle in the United States can be expensive and time-consuming. Undoubtedly, this leaves Mexico with little choice but to continue to buy the Genetic seeds. These purchases result in a deepening the poverty level of the country as more farmers are forced into bankruptcy because they cannot buy the seeds. The net result of this is that American companies have maximized their profitability by creating a new market in Latin America. It is estimated that this new industry will generate some $19 billion over the next 10 to 15 years. The system of Capitalism has worked effectively by allowing the surplus technology and funds of the American business community to be directed to a new market in Latin America. Consequently, as American corporations tapped the manufacturing and agricultural markets of Latin American, they are creating large pools of cheap labor which cannot find work there. These workers have become the surplus which Latin America must use to exploit markets in the rest of the world, predominantly the United States.

Mexico does not have large, well-funded corporations that can tap the American market and provide additional income flows, but Mexico does have a growing population of cheap, unemployed labor. These labor forces come from collapsed farming communities or individuals from cities coming to seek benefit in North America. If these people stay in

Mexico, they are a source of irritation and instability to the Mexican government. There is little infrastructure to support them in Mexico. As a result, the Mexican government has taken a rational attitude toward these surplus items: they use them as a business model to increase economic cash flows to Mexico. Foreign aid flowing into Mexico is less than $1 billion a year. If we add to that amount foreign investment of approximately $16 billion per year, the total becomes little less than $17 billion each year to Mexico. Those numbers quickly become dwarfed by the proceeds sent back to Mexico from illegal immigration into the United States. Since 2002, the amount sent by these immigrants has exceeded $20 billion and was second only to petroleum as a generator of revenue for the country. In many cases, entire Mexican villages will send their male populations to the United States to work and send money back to the villages in Mexico. It is little wonder that Mexico does very little to stop illegal immigration and takes an active role as a participant in fostering it. In the last 20 years, the money provided by these immigrants has become a vital source of revenue for the Mexican government. This is not to say that Mexico has done anything wrong. Quite the contrary, Mexico has learned to utilize Capitalism effectively.

Where Mexico does not have corporations to send and invest in North America, it does have millions of sole proprietors. These small economic engines are self-sustaining, self-motivating, and highly profitable. One such example was recently cited in the *Seattle Times*. An enterprising immigrant, using resources generated in the United States, returned to Mexico and began a small business selling pickled cactus. After five years of struggle and hard work and money obtained from her time in the U.S. as well as funds sent by her husband working in the U.S., a new factory rose from the dust of an abandoned cornfield in one small village in Mexico. Using the few resources they had, they created a new business selling the prickled cactus to health food stores around the world.

As a result of Mexico's brilliant use of sole proprietors in lieu of corporations, it is creating a very profitable and very broad-based structure of entrepreneurship, which provides a significant cash flow stream to the Mexican government. It should not be a surprise to anyone why the current president of Mexico uses every opportunity to encourage people to go from Mexico to the U.S. and to discourage the politicians in the United States from taking punitive measures against them. This is one of the most significant unintended consequences of globalization to yet be seen. Wherever technology and wealth have pooled in surplus in a particular country, the stratification engendered by globalization has also created poverty to balance it in some part of the world. This poverty is not a void but a different type of surplus, cheap labor, which this system will then try to move to where it is needed. This is truly an unexpected and unanticipated consequence of globalization.

The Future

It is our ability to understand the universe and the world around us which separates humanity from other species, or so we have been taught. Yet often what we have learned is corrupted with political correctness and fanciful ideas. For countless years, humanity saw the only way of dealing with weather was to control it. This effort was what started Edward Lorenz on his track leading to the creation of his no famous attractor and opening the doorway to a more comprehensive understanding of natural systems. We understand now we cannot control the weather but we can understand it and use information to help us minimize the damage it can cause. We have focused our attention on production tools rather than methods of control. We must then take the same approach in our effort to understand other natural systems that have global import.

Capitalism is not an economic model created by human beings, but is a natural system evolving all around human beings with the ability to survive and to propagate itself from society to society. This ability to propagate has enabled it to expand into a global system, affecting every culture and nation on the face of this planet. Its survival is a testament to the resilience of the system and its ability to adapt to changing conditions. Its ability to adjust can be seen in its evolution from a simple agrarian system to one that could accommodate industrialization and the massive changes it caused globally, to a highly complex and technical transport system distributing surplus information, technology, products, and culture around the world. As a complex, self-propagating, and sustaining natural system, Capitalism has traits and mechanisms which are independent of human beings. Like with weather, it is probably more beneficial to develop tools to understand and to forecast predicted changes in Capitalism rather than attempting to control it. Capitalism is the force which is shaping human culture. We need to direct our energies toward understanding the system and being able to create predictors of how the system will evolve in the future. When I talk about control, I'm referring to such efforts as attempts by individual governments to regulate immigration. People are nothing more than another commodity which the system seeks to distribute. We cannot stop this exchange because to do so would destroy the very system itself; it is a natural progression of the system. People are commodities and the system will work to distribute them as they are needed. This principle is already accepted by many governments but not by the populations within individual nations. We must also understand that boundaries created by governments will prove ineffective to restricting the flow of material as the system seeks to create equilibrium by distributing surplus to where it is needed. Understanding how the global system works is far more productive for humanity than attempting to defeat it. There are fundamental questions that we need to answer about the system to understand how we can best survive with it in the future.

Already we can see the first signs of a new stage of evolution as the system moves to accommodate global communications which transport technology and ideas in today's world. These systems have created a new degree of interconnection within the global system that we have yet to fully understand. We do know that the interconnection has made it possible to level the playing fields so that developed countries and developing countries have equal access to this information. It is making it possible for countries such as China and India to compete effectively against the developed countries of the U.S., France, Great Britain, and the rest of the Western world. It is forcing countries such as Russia and China to move away from ideology and to accept the reality of a global system which is independent of political concerns. As the field of opportunity has become more level, larger segments of the global population are finding it easier to gain access. It is no longer simply a Western phenomena based upon economic preference which drives globalization. People have become the single greatest driving force for the global system. Each individual has becalmed a point of connection within the system, exchanging information on technology, ideas, and culture on a global basis. Consequently, countries with larger populations are having a more significant impact than ever before. We need to understand how this impact will affect the global system and cause it to change. Understanding where the system is going may mean the difference between a stable global environment and one that is chaotic and destructive.

The advanced evolution of large natural systems is not limited to Capitalism. While Capitalism has been a major driving force for humanity, is has also been a driving force for the creation and development of other large natural systems. One of those we discussed earlier: the information systems, or the Internet. Here, technology driven by the needs of Capitalism has created a complex and sophisticated system designed to transport information globally. This functionality has been discussed by a number of authors and scholars, and the importance of this impact has been heralded by presidents and technocrats. The recent work in this area discussing how technology has leveled the playing field between developing countries and developing countries was written by the *New York Times* columnist, award-winning writer Thomas L. Friedman. In his book *The World Is Flat*, Freedman takes us through the stages of development for technology. He touches on the development of software innovations and the use of open-sourcing to allow the proliferation of the software. Making software systems available and keeping information flow open between developers in different areas and different countries has been a significant factor in the way the Internet has spread. Along with these developments came the inevitable reduction in pricing which results when developed countries invest money in technology in developing countries. The result of this is often the explosion of cheap labor in the developing countries. This cheap labor contracts more capital and investment as businesses understand the benefit to their bottom line, or profit, of using this cheap labor to reduce overall cost.

Once again, we can see the process envisioned by Richard Dawkins in the cultural transmission of ideas which he called memes. Free-trade is the rallying cry of thought for business interests as they explored this new system and its impact upon our society. The Internet has become an information clearinghouse not only for development of new technologies, but for the creation of new cultural mediums of expression. There are now sites on the Internet which came into existence for the single purpose of allowing individual expression through this medium. One of the most noble and controversial of the sites is Myspace.com. From its inception only a few years ago, it has become an overwhelmingly popular site used by individuals as a way of expressing themselves and sharing that expression with their peer groups. The Internet has fostered a new method of public discourse. For many in Generation Y, the use of digital technology as a medium of expression is as common place as dialogue was to Baby Boomers. Text messaging, file sharing, and info sourcing are common terms to this generation. I remember discussing this issue in one of my classes recently and finding many of the older students just as confounded and confused as I had been a few years ago about this new method of discourse. They found it incredible that their children would much prefer to text message each other even when sitting in the same room rather than to engage in conversation. It was only after some discussion that the older members of the class began to realize that text messaging afforded these young people not only an opportunity to engage in discourse but gave them more sense of empowerment as they engaged in communication in a controlled and restricted fashion, keeping it away from the prying eyes and ears of adults. It is this sense of empowerment that often attracts the young to the technology of the Internet.

The Internet is not the only technology to be spawned some by Capitalism as it has expanded and evolved in close contact with humanity. One of the most interesting and dynamic systems to evolve around Capitalism is that of monetary exchange. The study of Capitalism is always very closely associated with the study of the money. At all phases of the evolution of Capitalism did the need for exchange also create the necessity for a portable medium with which to create the exchange. An interesting article that I have run across concerning monetary evolution was written by Glyn Davies, "The History of Money from Ancient times to the Present". It provides a rather credible and entertaining overview of the history of money in Western society. As Mr. Davies points out, the use of money evolved from an expanding sense of custom and usage in the earliest years of human civilization. As cultural exchange was taking place between other societies and the growing system of Capitalism, the need to exchange surplus engendered the creation of portable units to facilitate this transaction. The first examples of money may have started simply with the exchange of quantities of grains or other foodstuffs, or perhaps exchange of animals, tools, or simple services to help collect food or animals was the first medium of exchange in a monetary sense; we may never know for sure. We do recognize that early forms of monetary exchange were simple barter systems that came into existence along with the agrarian system of Capitalism. Over time, the system of barter, which was somewhat cumbersome and difficult to maintain over long distances from the source material, prompted the evolution toward more sophisticated systems of exchange as communities move toward towns and cities. Davies is quick to point out that the use of banking came into existence long before the development of coins as a means of monetary expression. Banking reached a high level of sophistication in Egypt and regions of the Middle East long before the development of coinage. Davies also points out that military conquests were the primary vehicles for the development and spread of coinage as the military systems needed compact and efficient ways to pay soldiers.

We could spend a more exhaustive study of the history of money, but for the purposes of our work here, we simply need to move forward to the time of the 17th century when humanity, Capitalism, and monetary systems underwent a very significant change. The 1700s marked a period of time when we not only saw the creation of the first strong central governments in much of the Western world but also the emergence of central banks. It was during and this particular period of time that philosophers began to discuss the nature of money. David Hume, a philosopher, was one of the first to theorize about a qualitative theory of money, at the time where establishing a direct proportionality between goods and services in an economy and attaching to that a monetary value were important. The evolution of the central bank in England and its history for the creation of the coinage used in exchange and trade was to become the standard not only for Western world but for all civilizations.

As this vehicle of printed money took hold, it would be sometime before the true nature of the relationship between moneys being produced in different countries could be fully appreciate. The monetary system was well on its way toward devolving into a complete natural system in conjunction with Capitalism. If a maker or bread wanted to buy a pair of shoes, he no longer had to find a cobbler who was in need of a loaf of bread to complete the transaction. In the developing world of the 17th and 18th century, he simply took the state-generated coinage he received in exchange for his goods and used it to buy other commodities with complete safety.

In 1700s and 1800s, monetary systems were in their infancy and there was a little regard for how the systems interact with each other. It will not be until the end of the 1800s and into the early years of the 1900s that we have begun to see the evolution of the system and how it relates to other growing monetary systems all around the world. The first examples of using the currency of one nation to affect change or profit in the currency of another nation were seen just prior to World War I. However, these efforts were small and limited. This new enterprise prize was largely interrupted by three significant events before it could become a large-scale. The first was World War I which interrupted supplies of currency and commodities globally because of tariffs being imposed by many Western nations to protect their wealth and economies. This was a theory espoused at the time by Adam Smith in his work *The Wealth of Nations*. The second defendant was the resultant economic crash, or Depression, created by the World War I, and the use of tariffs by countries during this period of time. The amount of time it took for the world to move out of the Depression was marked by a second global conflict, World War II. But by then, economists and governments were becoming aware of the evolution of a monetary system and the need to protect the system for global stability. It was in this regard that the nations came together in 1947 in Breton Woods, New Hampshire, and created GATT, the General Agreement on Tariffs and Trade. While the name may be somewhat misleading, GATT did deal with tariffs and trade but also placed controls upon monetary systems. Government began to recognize that the movement of large amounts of currency across international boundaries created instability. In an effort in to ensure stability in monetary systems, the nations of the worlds decided to peg all currencies to the U.S. dollar.

The U.S. dollar to was to be the benchmark currency for all countries in the world for the next several decades. With the United States's preeminent position, their monetary systems created stability of all monetary systems for a short period of time. It is worthwhile to note that during this time, most currencies were backed by bimetallism: gold and silver. This backing of monetary units with precious metals would prove to be untenable just 20 years later as the European nations, having rebuilt their economies after World War II, were now interested in breaking their currencies away from the dollar to get more of a range in the value for the International Monetary Systems. This resulted in the abandoning of the GATT accord on Monetary Exchange and the establishment of a new accord called the Smithsonian Agreement in the 1970s. This agreement allowed European currencies to establish a value for their currencies in a degree of independence from the U.S. dollar, but did not completely disconnect these currencies from the dollar. Also during this period, the use of bimetallism was under attack globally as many more governments were moving toward information evaluation of monetary systems as a true measure of the worth of countries' money as opposed to the amount of gold and silver reserves being held by that country.

The Smithsonian Accord and the pressure on monetary systems for the removal of bimetallism resulted in the failure of those accords in less than 20 years. The result was a monetary system that we see today based upon information technologies, established productivity, economic capacity to, and a range of other indicators which established the value of an independent currency for any country.

All currencies in conjunction with each other create their own value based upon what the global monetary markets dictate. Monetary systems have evolved into a complex, sophisticated system of evaluating the worth of monetary units for the world's nations on a global basis. It is extremely closely tied to Capitalism. The five major currencies of the International Monetary Exchange are almost all based in Western countries. They are the U.S. dollar, the British pound, the Euro, the Japanese yen, and the Swiss frank. The Euro is a relatively new currency created out of the formation of the European Union. This system of monetary exchange moves trillions of dollars of surplus monetary units in trades all around the globe on a daily basis. The theory behind these exchanges is that currencies that are allowed to float in value can be viewed as a commodity and priced to make profit based upon the time-value of money. This system has created an industry which is 40 times the size of the existing U.S. Stock Market. As the monetary system grows in complexity and sophistication, it is attracting more and more efforts and concerns by central banks for control and monitoring. It is truly a global system that has significant impact upon the economic well-being of every citizen.

Recently, there has been speculation that the U.S. dollar must be adjusted against other world currencies. This is a good thing if you are a manufacturer trying to sell U.S. goods in the global marketplace because it means that your goods will now be cheaper and therefore more attractive as compared to other goods. However, this is not a good development for a worker in the United States being paid for his or her work in dollars. The decline in the value of the dollar means that the U.S.'s purchasing power in the global marketplace is less. In an age where economies are so interconnected that much of what the average citizen buys will come from other countries means the American worker will be able to afford less and that his work is valued less.

Still, this system allows developing countries an important tool to use in gaining access to the global marketplace. As Western currencies are valued more highly and currency from developing countries more cheaply, the developing countries will have an advantage in terms of attracting companies because of the cheaper materials and cheaper labor as valued by their cheaper currency. Evolution of natural systems, in conjunction with Capitalism, create a degree of complexity, sophistication, and variety which will continue to alter our world well into the next century.

Our search to understand natural systems such as Capitalism has led to an expansion of our own field of knowledge about these systems. We have developed new tools which have helped us not only in this area but in many other areas, expanding our field of knowledge significantly. In the 1970s when Benoit Mandelbrot first coined the word " fractal", no one knew exactly how far reaching its impact would be. Fractals are the fundamental building blocks used to create complex representations of natural systems. These visual representations give us a feeling of the complexity created from a simple constructs, the fractal. The beautifully complex images we have created on page are examples of complex structures that can be generated by simple and unique fractals. Each image can be reproduced by simply understanding the specific fractal which serves as the building block for the entire image. This concept has created a new and novel way of looking at very complex natural systems. One of the most important examples is that of the shoreline when viewed from space. From a far distance, the shoreline looks like a smooth and continuous surface. But as we increase magnification, we begin to see that the shoreline is composed of irregular features in a very complex pattern. This complex pattern can consume a great deal of computer memory which is necessary to reproduce the pattern in a visual image, or picture. In today's world, the study of complex systems has begun to lead researchers to consider the use of fractals as a way of creating image compressions that will allow large amounts of visual data to be transmitted very efficiently. If you can create the fractal image for a specific plant, you do not need to transmit volumes of data to recreate the image of the plant each time; you simply transmit the fractal, and the computer can recreate that particular plant from its unique fractal. Currently, there are a number of projects under way within the government and in private industry utilizing this method in image compression. This teaches us a new way of identifying specific unique factors which help understand the complexity of natural systems. From the patterns of conflict between different human societies, to the diseases which plague humanity, to the complexity of traffic information patterns in the global Internet, we find these natural systems on a daily basis in today's world. If we can eliminate the complexity and identify the specific fractal for them, we would be able to understand how the systems came into being, continue in their existence for some indeterminate period of time, and propagate themselves within our cultural broth. The understanding of these factors will perhaps lead us to an analysis of other important issues related to energy management and energy transmission.

By understanding the simple, we can now begin to see how to understand the complex. In a world of growing complexity, the need to reduce our analysis to some fundamental simplicity becomes essential. As we move into the future, with populations in our global environment exceeding

6.5 billion people, we will see the emergence of natural systems of varying durations and complexity. Understanding and being able to adequately analyze the systems will mean the difference between our civilization surviving or going the way of so many other civilizations who did not understand the complex natural systems in which they existed. We must begin to formulate our approach to deal with the systems in the same way that a surfer approaches his craft. We worked in harmony with the larger and more powerful systems rather than trying to oppose and to control them. We have to understand that humanity is not a culture of dam builders seeking to restrict and control systems. In very limited cases, we're able to do this to some degree. In the vast majority of natural and complex systems, our ability to control them is nonexistent. We must learn instead to live in harmony with them and to understand them. This provides a greater degree of success and benefit to humanity.

The natural system Capitalism has altered the way we look at fundamental concepts of wealth over the years. Earlier in this book, we discussed the concept of agrarian Capitalism and how its initial existence was attributed to the surplus generated by farming. Surplus is the primary factor which has reshaped Capitalism at several crucial periods. It is important to know at this juncture that Capitalism does not recognize surplus as wealth only; this natural system recognizes surplus in several different forms. During the age of agrarian expansion, surplus was measured in the production of output from farms, but it was also measured in the creation of another kind of surplus, cheap labor, as farming displaced other types of enterprises and moved large numbers of workers into the farming community. In a simple sense, farming was the better system and displaced other systems that were in competition with it. From these early stages, the system began to recognize surplus in terms that were irrelevant to today's concepts of wealth. The system has begun to recognize surplus not only as excess of goods, but also in terms of access personnel who could be readily identified as cheap labor. This particular concept became amplified as we moved into the age of industrialization where England took a decided advantage over its rivals in Europe as the three commodities of cheap labor, abundant coal resources, and the steam engine collided to produce new types of surplus in quantities the system had not had to deal with before. This prompted Capitalism to evolve into a new type of system capable of handling this surplus. This process was exported as both the production of goods and the existence of sources of cheap labor from immigrants led Europeans to emulate it in the New World. Capitalism was exporting both types of surplus it needed to keep its self moving and operating.

There is often a discussion of Capitalism creating pockets of poverty. It is this discussion that pits the forces of Capitalism against other social systems. This type of discussion is erroneous because Capitalism does not recognize social status, only surplus. For this natural system, surplus goods and surplus people are treated the same. Poverty is nothing more than surplus cheap labor to this system. It is nothing more than an imbalance within the system which it attempts to move to locations where it can be used in some type of exchange. This process will happen countless numbers of times in every part of the world today. During the age of agricultural systems, the process was not so pronounced because of the pace of a more leisurely type of social environment. As industrialization got under way, the process of creating these two extremes of surplus became amplified along with the pace of industrialization. It was Capitalism's ability to adjust to changes in type and quantity of surplus that has allowed it to survive and to proliferate among human societies. Yet, the system does not create poverty and/or exulted social status; it simply creates surplus in different forms.

We also come to a realization that Capitalism evolved more rapidly in Europe after the 12th and 13th century than it did in other parts of the world that were more populous, such as India and China. Daniel Cohen, in his book *Globalization and Its Enemies*, provides several explanations as to why this occurred. He points to the fact that until we reached the 12th and 13th centuries, there was relative parity between Europe and the rest of the world in terms of productive output and technological development. There was, however, a slight advantage to China in terms of technical development. Whereas Europe had created aqueducts to control water, they never effectively used hydroelectric power until we reach the modern age. Likewise, China had a highly developed sense of law, engineering, and chemistry well in advance of Europe. However, as we discussed earlier, a country may be the beneficiary of a technological advance, or several, but technology is not the sole province of any particular group of people. Random chance will often dictate where a technological advance will occur. However, once an advance occurs, it does not take long for the technology, or meme, to transmit itself to other cultures and to be adopted if it is a superior system. Over a period of time, this will often move other countries to catch up in technology to the original discovering country. In the case of China and India, decisions were made, as Daniel Cohen points out in his book, by those societies to turn inward and to engage in isolationism which separated them from the cultural flow of other societies. This isolationism disrupted the process for meme transmission, which would normally occur and allow their cultures to receive new ideas in exchange with other cultures and to eventually seek advancement through this exchange. Once again, we see the fundamental concept of governments and societies interfering with the evolution of the natural system and how these consequences can result in unexpected disadvantages. As a result of the isolation, these two large areas, as well as parts of South America and Africa, fell behind

Europe in the race for technology. By the time these societies were again breached by other cultures in the expansion of European and American influences known as colonialism, they where still primarily agricultural societies and not industrial societies. But, as Capitalism was introduced the system, it found usable surpluses that would fit well and were utilizable by the natural system. The surplus that was recognized was an abundant source of cheap labor.

This capability of Capitalism to use different types of surplus and to move them effectively throughout its system continues today. As we look around the global marketplace, Capitalism can be identified both by economic, military, and technological wealth in the industrial world and by an abundance of cheap labor in the developing world. Both these sources of surplus are acted upon by Capitalism to remedy the imbalance they cause within that system. As Western technology and money are moved toward the developing countries in an attraction to cheap materials and labor, so, too, is cheap labor attracted to Western countries as a place where that labor can be most effectively utilized. This does not mean that the laborers always have to leave the developing world to be fully utilized; they can be effectively utilized by the process known as off-shoring or outsourcing. As they are utilized, there is an effective exchange of surplus occurring so that the system can create a balance.

Industrialized countries are now finding that the

developing countries are beginning to catch up in terms of technology and wealth as the exchange engendered by Capitalism begins to take place. But, as always, Capitalism as a system needs the creation of surplus for it to exist. That surplus is not just wealth but also poverty. It is this anomaly of Capitalism that we must understand as being part of the overall system and to strip away the emotional rhetoric attached to it if we are to effectively understand the system and how it works. This will be the difference between making this system as efficient and as useful to humanity as possible or disrupting it as we have done in the past to the detriment of the global community.

Notes

Introduction

The Small ripple begins

Ehernberg, couched her discussion in terms of women and their participation in the movement of humans from foragers to stable farming communities. This process was fundamental in the creation of the first stable, long term settlements in the Fertile Crescent. She recognized that there were other sites where this process may have started, such as in Europe proper, or parts of Asia. It is this self organizing principle which is of fundamental importance. Her work is well worth reading for the insights it provides into the behavior of early human activities. "*Women in Prehistory*", by Margaret Ehrenberg , Oklahoma Series in Classical Culture, University of Oklahoma Press, Norman and London, 1989.

The discussion of such complexity leads directly to Chaos Theory. The introductory book by James Gleick was a good source of information to track down the discussion of using this theory with population problems. Gleick's book led to Robert M. May and his work on complexity in model eco-systems.

This defining principals of self-organization; excess, distribution of the excess, and system benefit of stability comes, out of the studies of the fireflies and oscillators in the new science of synchronous behavior. What is so fascinating is its application to either biological or non-biological systems. Equally as interesting is the discussion of why we as humans tend to miss such connections. Our minds are focused on linear solutions using straight forward logic of cause and effect.

The use of rhythm, and density is a fascinating look at the chemistry of bio-chemical systems. The story of trapping fireflies and putting them in a darkened hotel room to observe this phenomenon is wonderful. My first thought was of how hotel management must have felt about this, and then what did they do with the fireflies afterward.

The direct quotes from Ehrenberg,"*Women in Prehistory*", pages 86 and 89 respectively

Jared Diamond quote is from page 105 of his book, "*Guns, Germs, and Steel*"

Tipping points was first used by Morton Grozdins, "Metropolitan segregation", Scientific American 197, 1957, October.

The small world model was a social science creation of Stanley Milgram in his ground breaking studies of power and control in social settings. The experiment every on remembers is of people administering electrical shocks to encourage memory retention.

The evolution of economic theory by Adam Smith would drive the way economist viewed the system of Capitalism for decades, and influence modern economic thought. Smith intuitively recognized the existence of a natural system at work when he made reference to an invisible guiding hand controlling the process. It would be many years later, with the advent of Chaos Theory, and Sync, that suitable theories would exist to allow us to correctly categorize the system.

The Ripple Becomes a Wave

Transistors were the initial phase in a vast technological revolution. In a matter of decades it would create computers for the desk top, and hand held units for the storage of music, and video. This revolution would be the platform for the last stage of capitalism, the global system.

Social reform brought about by unions would lead to the first stages of revolt against the rapid changes of global capitalism. Although unions would decline, their impact on the social consciousness of the nation would be long lived

The System at Maturity

Author Index

A

Albert, R., Jeong, H., and Barabasi, A.L., “Anatomy of the World Wide Web”, *Nature* 401, 1999, pages 309-320

Annan, Kofi, “We the Peoples: The Role of the United Nations in the 21st Century”, Secretary general of the United nations, For the Millennium Summit, 2000

B

Bridis, Ted, “Arab Firm May Run 6 U.S. Ports”, *Seattle Times* February 12, 2006

Baumam, Zygmunt, “*Globalization”*, Columbia UP, 1998

Bender, B., “*Farming in Prehistory”*, John Baker London, 1975

Bender, B., “Gather-Hunter to Farmer: A Social Perspective”, *World Archaeology* 10 Pages 204—222, 1978

Billis, Mary, “*Inventors of the Modern Computer Series: The History of the Transistor”, John Bardeen, Walter Brattain, and William Shockley*, **2004**

Binford, L. R., “*In Pursuit of the Past”*, Thames and Hudson, London, 1983

Boudreaux, Richard, “Mexican’s U.S. Wages Fuel Dream”, *Seattle Times Close UP*, Sunday April 30, 2006

Buck, John, “Synchronous Rhythmic Flashing of Fireflies”, *Quarterly Review of Biology* 13, 1938 (pages 301-314)

Buck, John, and Buck, Elisabeth, "Mechanism of Rhythmic Synchronous Flashing of Fireflies", *Science*, 159, 1968—page 1319-1327

C

Cohen, Daniel, "*Globalization and Its Enemies*", The MIT Press, pages 111- 160, 2006

D

Davies, Glyn., " A History of Money from Ancient Times to the Present Day", 3rd. ed. Cardiff: University of Wales Press, 2002.

Diamond, Jared, "*Guns, Germs, and Steel: The Fates of Human Societies*", Norton, 1999

Diamond, Jared, "*Collapse: How Societies Choose to Fail or Succeed*", Penguin Books, 2005

Dyson, T., "*Population Growth and Food Production: Recent Global and Regional Trends*." Population and Development Review (20)2: 403. 1994

E

Ehernberg, Margaret, *Women in Prehistory*, Oklahoma Series in Classical Culture, University of Oklahoma Press, Norman and London, 1989. Chapter 3

F

Frieden, Jeffery A., "*Global Capitalism*", W.W. Norton and Company New York, 2006

Friedman, Thomas L., "*The World Is Flat*", Farrar, Straus and Giroux, New York, 2005.

Fruedenheim, Milt, “The Next Retirement Time Bomb”, *New York Times*, December 11, 2005

G

Gleick, James, “*CHAOS: The Making of a New Science”*, Penguin Books, 1989- pages 11-39

Gladwell, Malcom, “*The Tipping Point”*, Little, Brown and Company, 2002

H

Holly, David, “Russia, China Join to Demand Autonomy”, *Los Angles Times*, reprinted in *Seattle Times*, July 2, 2005

J

Jowitt, Kenneth, “*The New World Disorder”*, Berkeley : University of California Press, 1992.

K

Kuramato, Y, “Self-entrainment of a Population of Coupled Nonlinear Oscillators”, *International Symposium on Mathematical Problems in Theoretical Physics*, edited by H. Araki pp 420-422

Kuhn, Thomas S., *The Structure of Scientific Revolutions,* The University of Chicago Press, 1962

L

Laurent, Phillip, “The Supposed Synchronous Flashing of Fireflies”, *Science* 45, 1917

Lowenstien, Roger, “We Regret to Inform You That You No Longer Have a Pension”, *New York Times Magazine*, October 30, 2005

M

Mandelbrot, Benoit, “*The Fractal Geometry of Nature*, New York: Freeman”, 1977

May, Robert M, “*Stability and Complexity in Model Ecosystems”*, Princeton UP, 1973, 1974

McClintock, Martha K, “Menstrual Synchrony and Suppression”, *Nature* 228, 1971, pages 244-245

McNeil, J.R., and Kennedy, Paul, “*Something New Under the Sun”*, by Norton 2001

Mellaart, J., "T*he Neolithic of the Near East*, Thames and Hudson", London, 1975

MEWREW. ," *Middle East and Africa Water Review"*, London: SOAS Water Issues Group, http://www.soas.ac.uk/geography/waterissues/. 1995.

Milgram, Stanley,"*The Individual in a Social World: Essays and Experiments"*, McGraw Hill
1992

Moore, Molly, “I Never Imagined… This in Paris” *Washington Post*, reprinted in the *Seattle Times*, March 24, 2006

Morris, Ruth, “Cuba Trades Doctors for Oil in Unique Payment Plan”, *South Florida Sun-Sentinel*, reprinted in *Seattle Times*, December 21, 2005

S

Smale, Steven J., "*The Mathematics of Time: Essays on Dynamical Systems, Economical Processes, and Related Topics"*, New York: Springer-Verlag, 1980, pages 147-151

Smith, Hugh, "Synchronous Flashing of Fireflies", *Science* 82, 1935—pages 151-152

Smith, Adam, "*An Inquiry into the Nature and Causes of the Wealth of Nations"*, Published: London: Methuen and Co., Ltd., ed. Edwin Cannan, 1904. Fifth Edition. First Published 1776

T

Thompson, Tom, "Why They Come Here", *Seattle Times FOCUS*, Sunday May 21, 2006

, "Warning Raised About Exodus Of Philippine Doctors and Nurses", *New York Times International Section*, November 27, 2005

U

Uchitelle, Louis, "For Blacks a Dream in Decline", *New York Times*, October 23, 2005

Uchitelle, Louis, "Two Tiers, Slipping into One " *The New York Times*, February 26, 2006

W

Wood, Ellen Meiksins, "The Agrarian Origins of Capitalism", *Monthly Review*, 1998

Woods, Ellen, Meiksins, "*The Origin of Capitalism: A Longer View"*, Verso, 2002

Winfree, Arthur, "Biological Rhythms and the Behavior of Populations of Couple Oscillators" .*Journal of Theoretical Biology* 16 (1967), pages15- 42.

Y

Yorke, James A., and Li, Tien-Yien, “Period Three Implies Chaos”, *American Mathematical Monthly* 82, 1975, pages 985-992

ARTICLES

National Academies Press release, "Broad Federal Effort Urgently Needed to Create New, High-Quality Jobs for All Americans in the 21st Century", October 12, 2005

United Nations Environmental Project, "Global Environment Outlook 2000"

SUBJECT INDEX

www.ingramcontent.com/pod-product-compliance
Lightning Source LLC
Chambersburg PA
CBHW031553280326
41928CB00047BA/247